A guide to recent architecture

Vienna

Ingerid Helsing Almaas
Photographs by Keith Collie

Vienna

A guide to recent architecture

● ● ● ellipsis KÖNEMANN

•••

CREATED, EDITED AND DESIGNED BY
Ellipsis London Limited
55 Charlotte Road London EC2A 3QT
E MAIL ...@ellipsis.co.uk
www http://www.ellipsis.co.uk/ellipsis
PUBLISHED IN THE UK AND AFRICA BY
Ellipsis London Limited
SERIES EDITOR Tom Neville
SERIES DESIGN Jonathan Moberly
LAYOUT Pauline Harrison

COPYRIGHT © 1996 Könemann
Verlagsgesellschaft mbH
Bonner Str. 126, D-50968 Köln
PRODUCTION MANAGER Detlev Schaper
PRINTING AND BINDING Sing Cheong
Printing Ltd
Printed in Hong Kong

ISBN 3 89508 287 2 (Könemann)
ISBN 1 899858 02 4 (Ellipsis)

Ingerid Helsing Almaas 1995

Contents

Introduction

I am an outsider to Vienna. This guide is based on my visits to the city during the last eight years; as an architectural tourist, as a student, and most recently during three-months of intense research for this book.

I make no claims to being representative. Viennese architecture is very well documented in the impressive œuvre of numerous Austrian architectural writers. My selection starts from 1985, and is based on, and no doubt reflects, my personal likes and dislikes. I have not included one-family houses as these are often very difficult to visit. In an attempt to make my contact with the recent architecture of Vienna as broad as possible, my research has included talking to as many of the city's architects as I had time for. These conversations form part of the text of this book.

There is a lot of building currently going on in Vienna. A large proportion of it is publicly funded, and it is not least due to informed politicians, like current City Planning Councillor Hannes Swoboda, that building also can mean architecture. This is a relatively new development. During the 1960s and '70s most larger public commissions, including social housing, were given to large firms of architects with political affiliations. The flame of architecture was tended by a small number of people like Hans Hollein or Hermann Czech, whose work was limited to shop interiors for private clients, theoreticians like Friedrich Achleitner and Otto Kapfinger, or by Austrian architects who built a reputation for themselves abroad, in Germany or Switzerland, like Roland Rainer or Gustav Peichl. There was time, if not money, for a small minority to involve themselves in historical and theoretical research, and for groups like Haus-Rucker Company (Laurids Ortner and others), Missing Link (Kapfinger and Adolf Krischanitz), and Coop Himmelblau (Wolf Prix and Helmut Swiczinsky) to do art actions and installations. Most of these architects are still building, even if the groups have been dispersed, and a new generation of architects is rising to prominence alongside them, driven by the recent wave of informed commissioning which, according to many, started when Swoboda came to office in the City Hall to administer the large expansion projects which became necessary when the population of the city started to grow after decades of decline. However, Swoboda too had his models: there have been similar developments in other parts of Austria, in Graz and in Styria, where, depending on the personal initiatives of informed politicians, almost every major public commission has been allocated by open or invited competition.

Apart from the need to deal with a growing population, there are of course also political points to be scored. Any housing project which sports the inscribed plaque of the Gemeinde Wien inevitably also mentions the name of the mayor of Vienna, Helmut Zilk. Zilk is no. 1 on the gossip magazine *News*' list of the 500 most important people in Austria, followed closely by Bundeskanzler Franz Vranitzky and Arnold Schwarzenegger as a good no. 3. Interestingly, the list also includes some architects: Wilhelm Holzbauer (no. 43, up from last year's 240), Hans Hollein (no. 63, down from 29), Gustav Peichl (no. 123), Roland Rainer (no. 276, up from 434), Coop Himmelblau (no. 323) and Klaus Kada (no. 445, a newcomer on the list). City Councillor for Planning, Hannes Swoboda, clocks in at no. 177.

However obvious and superficial such lists are, they say something about the public's perception of architects in Austria. In Britain, which by way of comparison has more than ten times as many people, you would do well to find more than two or three architects with any celebrity value. And even if this listing does not necessarily imply greater public understanding of architectural issues, it is interesting to note that the architects mentioned are not the heads of the big commercial practices with strong political connections but high-quality designers.

In the last ten years, or more precisely since as long as Swoboda has been in the post of City Planning Councillor, the appointment of good architects, of young architects, of non-party-affiliated architects, has become more common. It still applies only to some 10 per cent of the total output of the housing industry, but as politicians and big business alike have woken up to the fact that good architecture has a useful signal value, more architects are getting the chance to build. It is perhaps too much to hope that this commissioning has established itself as common practice among the housing associations – politicians are fickle creatures whose support is withdrawn as quickly as it is given – but one can only hope that the profession uses this opportunity to establish its position as a valuable resource for the city.

IHA: The relations between architecture and politics, or maybe rather between architects and politicians, seem to be quite close in Vienna at the moment?

Friedrich Achleitner (architectural historian and theoretician): At the moment it looks good, yes. But such things can change quickly when politicians are exchanged.

IHA: Do you think that the commissioning of young architects is established as a tradition among the housing associations, that it is not purely politically dependent?

Achleitner: Not established. It is just that the politicians in the meantime have understood that the Viennese model has become internationally known and discussed. I was with a group from Vienna in Kiel to present the Viennese housing construction situation, and you had the feeling that other cities in Germany, including Berlin, were looking to what was currently happening in Vienna. And that is of course interesting for the politicians, as they see that such a policy is made into a model and has an effect. So in as much as this is the case it can work in favour of architecture for a long time, but not necessarily. There is no guarantee. And it is surely not institutionalised.

IHA: How deeply does the understanding of architecture go? Is it the case that as far as the politicians are concerned, Hundertwasser is the same as Himmelblau?

Achleitner: For some politicians that is surely the case. The Mayor of Vienna is a bit of both, he has supported both Hollein and Hundertwasser. But it can of course also happen that it operates simply on the level of personal taste, which can be catastrophic.

In writing this book I have been looking for a publishable generality, for words to sell, a way to sum up, to circumscribe an outsider's view of the last ten years of Viennese architecture. I have not found it. Vienna is a city in the making, and because of the demographical changes of a growing population much more so than, for example, London, where I normally work. Different people are building different buildings, and though there is certainly political awareness, there is not the political will to force development in any particular qualitative direction.

Christian Knechtl (architect, Eichinger oder Knechtl): So what are you trying to write? Do you describe how the buildings could be seen, or several different approaches, or ... ?

IHA: I would like to write as little as possible. The things which interest me are buildings where you can just describe the facts, and the meaning

Vienna: a guide to recent architecture

gives itself.

Knechtl: What are the facts? That is subjective too, you have social facts, you have the facts of time …

IHA: I actually mean materials. My ideal is to be able just to describe how this material is placed next to that, and you immediately understand that it has an architectural meaning.

Knechtl: OK. You are describing the objects, not interpreting them.

IHA: No. I would like not to, but I also interpret.

A city develops slowly, it remembers and forms habits, in a process which cannot be directed by the abstractions of a strategic plan, however well-considered. Architects have a much more direct possibility to influence the details of that development, they can direct where people go, what they see, what they touch … I would like to come back to these projects in ten years and record the new habits of the city: only then will we as architects and planners be able to assess the success of our predictions.

Acknowledgements

I would like to thank all the architects as well as photographer Margherita Spiluttini and City Councillor Hannes Swoboda, for talking to me and patiently answering my questions, and for all the material they supplied. Thanks especially to Hermann Czech who took the time to correct my building list, to Walter Chramosta who does 30,000 kilometers a year throughout the country and really has an idea of recent Austrian building, to all friends in Vienna whose ears I bent night after night with my opinions on architecture, to Keith Collie for his patience in photographing it all, and to Simon for maintaining life in London all those evenings we could not be in Prückel.
IHA December 1994

Vienna: a guide to recent architecture

The guide divides the 23 districts of Vienna plus a couple of nearby towns into ten sections, grouping the buildings reachable by more-or-less the same lines of transport. The street address of each building is preceded by a number from 1 to 23 indicating the district or *Bezirk* it is in. The address is followed by a map co-ordinate which refers both to the standard public-transport plan, *Verkehrslinienplan*, available in all underground stations, and to the more detailed city maps by Freytag & Berndt. The *Verkehrslinienplan* is indispensable for making the most of Vienna's impressive public-transport system, but not great for finding smaller streets. If you are not keen on getting around by asking the locals, Freytag & Berndt's *Städteatlas* is a necessary supplement.

Public transport in Vienna is fantastic. From the centre you can get almost anywhere in the 23 districts within half an hour, and you rarely have to walk for more than ten minutes from any bus or tram stop to a particular address. The Viennese have got used to the service and complain incessantly about it, expecting buses carrying no more than five people to run every ten minutes to and from remote suburban destinations.

GETTING THERE assumes a starting point in the centre of the city and tells you which lines to catch and the names of the stations. All stations are announced well in advance, and for those unfamiliar with the Austrian accent they are written in at least three places on every stop, in addition to route plans both in the stations and inside all vehicles. Theoretically, with a little help from passers-by you could make do with no map at all, simply following the instructions given in this guide.

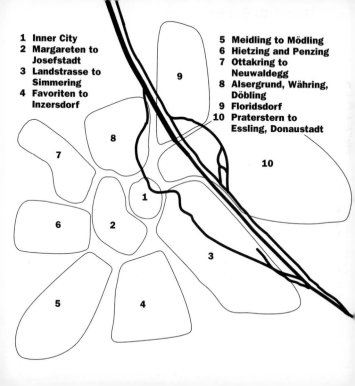

1 **Inner City**
2 **Margareten to Josefstadt**
3 **Landstrasse to Simmering**
4 **Favoriten to Inzersdorf**
5 **Meidling to Mödling**
6 **Hietzing and Penzing**
7 **Ottakring to Neuwaldegg**
8 **Alsergrund, Währing, Döbling**
9 **Floridsdorf**
10 **Praterstern to Essling, Donaustadt**

Housing Associations

EBG: Gemeinnützige Ein- und Mehrfamilienhäuser Baugenossenschaft

'FAMILIENHILFE' Gemeinnützige GmbH

'FRIEDEN' Gemeinnützige Bau- und Siedlungsgenossenschaft GmbH

GEMEINDE WIEN

GESIBA

GP: Genossenschaft der Privatangestellten

GSG: Gesellschaft für Stadtentwicklung und Stadterneuerung Gemeinnützige GmbH

GWV

'NEUES LEBEN' Gemeinnützige Bau-, Wohn- und Siedlungsgenossenschaft GmbH

'SCHÖNERE ZUKUNFT' Gemeinnützige Wohn- und Siedlungsgesellschaft

SEG: Stadterneuerungs- und Eigentumswohnungsgesellschaft mbH

ÖBV: Österreichische Beamtenversicherung

ÖS: Österreichische Siedlungswerk

WE: Wohnungseigentum Gemeeinnützige GmbH

WEVAG: Wohnpark Errichtungs- und Vermietungs Aktien Gesellschaft

WP: Wohnbauvereinigung für Privatangestellte Gemeinnützige GmbH

WOHNHAUSANLAGE WIENERBERG GmbH

Vienna: a guide to recent architecture

Inner City

The Haas-Haus is an easy building to criticise. Its profusion of materials and forms blows it wide open to charges such as inconsistency and confusion. However, one thing on which the critics agree is that the most astounding thing about the Haas-Haus is that it is there at all. In the most prestigious place in Vienna the politicians had the will to allow the erection of a thoroughly modern building, which makes no compromises to its historical neighbours, neither the medieval cathedral nor the neo-baroque of the late 19th century. It was funded by some of the most prestigious financial institutions of the city, and even when media criticism was at its hardest, the mayor of Vienna, Helmut Zilk, on whose personal initiative the project was started, did not waver in his support for Hollein's design.

Having said that, the design itself is hard to get to grips with.

IHA: With most other buildings that I am confronted with, I can feel some points of attachment, something I can understand or criticise – materially, organisationally, in relation to context, history, etc. With the Haas-Haus I have a real problem with that. Both what it is in itself, and where it is, there is such a profusion of things that I can't find anything to grab hold of somehow. Can you help?

Otto Kapfinger (architectural critic): Hollein could only do it this way. It was his way; you could not criticise Hollein for doing the Hollein-thing. We, the critics, had to support it; other people wanted to keep the old building which was not possible, you couldn't use it anymore.

For Hollein it was the chance of his life, a very difficult situation, and he wanted too much. He focused on the urbanistic problem, making a division between Stephansplatz and Stock-im-Eisen-platz with the balconies and the shapes coming out of the main form. Hollein

Hans Hollein 1990

Hans Hollein 1990

wanted to react to everything with his façade and I think it was too much, an over-exertion.

On postcards you usually see a view of the Haas-Haus and the Stephansdom together. This is not helpful in making sense of the building. The Haas-Haus sweeps around from the Graben; it comes from a world of shops, from polished granite and brass, and has only incidentally to do with that medieval mountain of stone.

It is not a particularly clever shopping centre. Because of the eccentricity of the interior to the exterior cylinder some of the shops along the outside become extremely shallow. You cannot see the upper floor shops from the outside. The entire top floor is taken up by a record store, which ensures a constant filtering of scruffy teenagers through all floors, preventing the desired exclusive atmosphere. The shops have little opportunity to swell and gleam like they do along the Graben. The building itself does the swelling, the interior hall is filled by a mountain of materials: marble, granite, stainless steel, aluminium, gold leaf, glass, neon lights – a veritable architectural boutique. The hall is a giant stage-set, where the escalators ascend between layers of stone towards the vanishing point of a false perspective, a few square metres of painted blue sky, the only escape.

But again, the Haas-Haus is easy to criticise. For whatever reason, whether it be the political circumstances of the commission or the personality of the architect, it gives you very few clues to any structure in its multitude of forms.

This, ironically, is perhaps the greatest challenge of the building: you are forced to decide upon a hierachy of your own, to choose for yourself how to understand it. I prefer the building just before dark, when the

Hans Hollein 1990

Inner City

Hans Hollein 1990

inside lights start to become visible, when other buildings and parts of the city sky are mirrored in the metal-coated glass, and the polished stone cladding glows with reflected light. All the gleaming facts of the building become uncertain, and different degrees of transparency break up the theatrical form and transparent glass, reflective glass, polished granite and stainless steel acquire a difference you don't see during the day.

ADDRESS 1., Stock-im-Eisen-Platz 4 [32 N 12]
CLIENT Kommerz-Real, Wiener Städtische Wechselseitige Versicherungsanstalt and 'Wiener Verein'
GETTING THERE U1 or U3 to Stephansplatz
ACCESS open

Hans Hollein 1990

Bibelwerk bookshop

The principle is very simple. Bookshelves. An old room directly behind the Stephansdom is filled with three new furniture-structures made from slender grey steel sections, precisely joined. The structure in the middle carries two levels of bookshelves and allows the upper parts of the white-washed walls and vaults to be left relatively bare. There are books everywhere, more like a library stack than a shop, and you can browse not only through books but also through the old space, on all levels of the bookshelf structures.

Details like spiral silk-covered light fittings give a disturbing feeling of familiarity, of a tension between old and new materials, old and new solutions which continues on the façade. The old building has been hung with framed sheets of varnished glass, red and purple, something halfway between shop-signs and cladding. Glass cases for book display extend the shop windows out on to the external wall with precise, slim joinery. The building simultaneously indulges and challenges the nostalgic traditions of the small Viennese Inner City shop.

The prime location has become problematic for the shop. The content, religious books, Christian theory, which is well served by Prochazka's concentrated design, is cluttered up with the predictable array of postcards of the Stephansdom and Gustav Klimt Christmas calendars trying to make the most of the tourist trade.

ADDRESS 1., Singerstrasse 7 [32 N 12]
CLIENT Österreichisches Katholisches Bibelwerk
SIZE 123 square metres
OTHER shortlisted for the Adolf Loos Prize for Architecture 1994
GETTING THERE U1 to Stephansplatz
ACCESS open

Elsa Prochazka 1991

Elsa Prochazka 1991

Wrenkh café and restaurant

To make an atmosphere is a question of associations. The interiors by Eichinger oder Knechtl suggest some but also always leave large blanks, areas to be filled by time, by use, and they provide a no-fuss material quality to match, which will keep the promise and stand by as time passes. Simple sheets of varnished plywood, corrugated aluminium sheet, a satin-finish stainless steel bar, in summer an orange rubber canopy stretched across the front.

There are surprising details, timed spotlights sweeping the façade of the building opposite, the glass phone box with a huge leather seat, the angle of the front. Yet there is something irritatingly correct about the design, a self-consciousness stretched tautly over it all – the little Campari-bottle lightshelf is as close to expression as you get, they toy with those old things but even then the risk of giving away too much is balanced by the satire of conscious kitsch – you can't fault them.

ADDRESS 1., Bauernmarkt 10 [32 N 12]
CLIENT Christian Wrenkh
GETTING THERE U1 or U3 to Stephansplatz
ACCESS open

Inner City

Eichinger oder Knechtl 1989

Eichinger oder Knechtl 1989

Restaurant Kiang

This interior is put together entirely from industrial or man-made materials: rubberised sheet, studded rubber floor, glassfibre moulded chairs, back-lit thermal plastic panels above the bar, stainless steel, a blue glass entrance door. Behind the red rubber sheet wall a blue laminate box in the corner contains the toilets, matt outside, polished within.

It is all screwed into the existing building as if it were to be taken out tomorrow; different materials are assembled and held together for a short while, in tension, on the way back to where they came from. However, in Vienna things tend to remain. Despite all the synthetic materials it still has the attributes, intended or acquired, of a Viennese bar or café – the materials, all good quality, have yellowed a bit, settled in, and in winter there are heavy curtains behind the door, the open coat-rack. Interestingly, it is being run as a Chinese restaurant, and not as a café.

In summer the aluminium sliding panel façade is open to the street; horizontally mounted roller blinds can provide screening if necessary. The plywood sheet ceiling slopes, as does the street outside. The front pillars of the existing building have been clad with yellow varnished plywood sheet, mirrors inside the openings. Strip lights at the head of each opening light the interior at night. The concentration of light at the street front turns the people eating their noodles by the windows into a strange but familiar theatre.

ADDRESS 1., Rotgasse 8 [32 N 12]
CLIENT Thomas Kiang
GETTING THERE U1, U4, or tram 1, 2 or N to Schwedenplatz
ACCESS open

Helmut Richter and Heidulf Gerngross 1985

Helmut Richter and Heidulf Gerngross 1985

Ron Con Soda

In winter when the front is closed this little bar takes on the atmosphere of a strange storage room off the street, full of heavy wooden furniture. The bar itself is a glittering wall of bottles at the end of the room, back-lit from the partly glazed concrete stair going up to the First Floor (see page 32). The feet of people going past and up adds to the sense of having found a place only incidentally connected to the routines of city life. The street outside slopes steeply up from Schwedenplatz and inside the whole of the floor is stepped, the tables have two legs cut short to stay level. In the summer the front is open and the street continues in, up the wooden steps right to the bar.

This place is made for drinking. Wherever you are standing or sitting there is some beautifully simple steel or aluminium detail at your elbow to hold your drink for you. The only question is whether you like rum, which is what they serve, and Cuban music, which is what they play.

ADDRESS 1., Rabensteig 5 [32 N 12]
CLIENT Michael Satke
GETTING THERE U1 or U4 to Schwedenplatz
ACCESS open

Inner City

Eichinger oder Knechtl 1994

First Floor

There used to be a very famous bar on the Kärntner Strasse called the Mounier Bar, frequented by the artists and writers of the 1930s. It was demolished recently, and pieces of the old interior were waiting to be thrown out when Michael Satke saw them and bought them. Eichinger oder Knechtl have used them to complete Satke's complex of bars in the Rabensteig, realising their vision of city ecology. The old interior panelling and furniture are combined with new materials in a process of recycling which makes the place look as if it has already been there for ten years but is still waiting for something new to happen.

The entrance is up the stairs above Ron Con Soda (another of Satke/Eichinger oder Knechtl's bars, next to the Roter Engel by Coop Himmelblau), across a piece of glass floor and through a small cell with mirrored sides, a disorientating hole in time where the only thing you can see is the reflection of the busy bartender floating in the black space. The bar itself is a tunnel of old and new veneered sheets, combined with beautifully precise joinery in all the details which frame the ritual of professional drinks-makery. The intention of the owner was to make a bar for people who did not want to go to other bars: the old interior, steeped in cultural tradition, is one of the subtle ways of screening the clientele. Go there after dark, when the only light comes through two large aquariums behind the bar: the First Floor is a pocket carved out of the fabric of the city, a finely crafted fabrication.

Gregor Eichinger: Eichinger oder Knechtl are a special office in Vienna, because we were really the first to work in different directions – graphics, design, architecture, city planning. We did the cover for *Falter* [weekly Vienna events guide] for a long time, which was interesting because it was like city-planning research for us. It was fun. We are

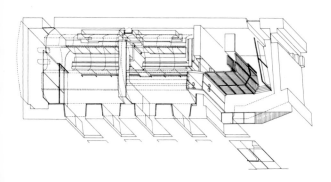

Eichinger oder Knechtl 1994

free to pick things from one place and apply them to another situation. If there is an obstacle in a certain direction we can go round and come from the back, from the other side. For us it is not so important to have an ideology in the way architects like to have, to have a manifesto – we have a manifesto but it's much more something like water. Floating, you know? We're moving, and we are doing several projects at the same time which are completely different, which are in different professional directions. But the thing is, we try to do it in an architectural way, not as architects are supposed to do them but as we think architects could act. So we are working on exhibitions, ones where we make the exhibition design but also one which is our exhibition, where the scientific research is completely done by us, and we have graphics, book covers, creating bars and living spaces, and a video project we started some time ago – this is just normal for us, it is a normal office schedule.

Christian Knechtl: So we are not doing a building but we do a newspaper, for example. We are starting a newspaper, or we do another party.

Eichinger: And the good thing is, there are only two of us but it looks like we are a crowd of Indians running around, and wherever they look, there we are. [Laughs]

Inner City

ADDRESS 1., Seitenstettengasse 1 [32 N 12]
CLIENT Michael Satke
GETTING THERE U1 or U4 to Schwedenplatz
ACCESS open

Eichinger oder Knechtl 1994

Eichinger oder Knechtl 1994

Unger & Klein wine shop

A small wine shop in a quiet area towards the back of the Inner City. The existing space is rendered and painted white, a background for a civilised theatre of drinking. The refinement is not in the materials, which are very simple: varnished furniture board, welded and galvanised steel frames made up of simple standard profiles, fairfaced concrete. There are small tables, Roland Rainer designed chairs, a tall leather sofa just inside the door. The wine bottles are stored and displayed in a full-height shelf which curves through to a smaller room at the back, lighting is from behind one shelf-row of empty green bottles. There is a concrete counter along the wall with a trough for rinsing and cooling bottles and a stainless steel tank for fresh wine at the end. The elegance is first of all in the way the shop is run: the mixture of buying and drinking, bottles of vinegar and pickled vegetables are displayed on the same table you are eating at, the back room which you would expect to be a store also has a big table which can be used for private parties, connected by a carefully placed mirror to the leather sofa. This unconventional mixture of functions is accommodated and underlined by the self-conscious simplicity of the design in which each element is intelligently considered and placed in relation to the others.

The shop front is covered by aluminium sliding doors with bottle-shaped cut-outs, where a few select bottles are on exhibit, ensuring you won't be disappointed even if you come here when the shop is closed.

ADDRESS 1., Gölsdorfgasse 2 [32 N 12]
CLIENT Michi Klein and Helmut Unger
GETTING THERE TRAM 1 or 2 to Salztorbrücke or U4 or U1 to Schwedenplatz
ACCESS open

Inner City

Eichinger oder Knechtl 1992

Eichinger oder Knechtl 1992

Atelier for a graphic artist

The façade of an old building facing a square in the Inner City gives three hints of a complex story. One is filled with aluminium, one with glass and one by a steel staircase. The story inside is that of a structure, an irregular assembly of thin steel members which brings the load of a workplace down to a single, very small point on the floor. Part of the structure penetrates the old façade.

IHA: Friedrich Achleitner has said that even the work of Coop Himmelblau can be placed within the context of an attraction to complexity and ambiguity which has been a specifically Viennese 'accompaniment to modernity'. (*Die rückwärtsgewandte Utopie: Motor des Fortschritts in der Wiener Architektur* [Picus Verlag, Wien 1994])

Prix: Yes ... you can only smuggle small things across rigid borderlines. If you come with a big thing, the guards are very protective of this border ... They are very accurate in controlling what you are smuggling. So if Himmelblau smuggled not only small things but big things, it means that now the guards are changing the borderline, stretching it around what was mistakenly allowed in, in order not to be blamed or embarrassed by the things that are now reality. So first they tried to say that it can not be built, and when it was built they blamed it. But this is a regular way to explain innovation in culture. When we showed a critic some of our work ten years ago he said: 'this is very ugly. I don't like it because it's so ugly'. The same critic said when we had the exhibition in the Pompidou: 'it's much too beautiful now'.

STRUCTURAL ENGINEER Oskar Graf
CONSTRUCTION Metallbau Treiber, Graz
ACCESS absolutely none

Inner City

Coop Himmelblau (Wolf Prix and Helmut Swiczinsky) 1985

Coop Himmelblau (Wolf Prix and Helmut Swiczinsky) 1985

Sigmund Freud Society Library

Because of a planned extension of the lecturing facilities, the library of the Sigmund Freud Society needed to change its existing single toilet into a double male and female facility and to build a second fire-escape stair.

The new toilets are set into the existing wall of a narrow corridor-space between two rooms, half inside the apartment, half hanging out the back into the lightwell, and painted pigeon grey. All the plywood components were made off site, and brought together to fill the hole in the existing wall. It all fitted precisely. Some of the finer steel parts were handcrafted by the architect. It makes no attempt to comment on Freud or his apartment: something simply happened to some sheets of plywood and now this thing stands there. The urinal flushes now and again, as well it should.

The new work to the library also includes bookshelves – floor-to-ceiling steel mesh shelves strung out on thin cable – and the reading table in the modest reading room. The table, also made by the architect, is a long self-supporting hollow fibreglass-reinforced resin U-section on steel trellises, slightly translucent and surprisingly temperate to the touch. The hushed precision of the materials is a curious presence in the hallowed surroundings of Sigmund Freud's former home: ponderous but refreshingly inconsiderate.

The fire-escape stair in the courtyard has never been used. It is made from the fascination of two lengths of steel, one I-section and one round section, which escort each other down until they almost touch the ground, where the end of the staircase is held up by a bracket bolted to the wall. Sideways movement of the structure is prevented by a hollow carbon-fibre prop stretched across the diagonal of the two crossing steel stringers. There are other ways, simpler ways of doing it, it doesn't have to be like this. But it is.

Additions Wolfgang Tschapeller 1991

Tschapeller told me about his work, and for two hours he spoke only about the materials, only the process of putting them together, no explanations, no interpretation: thought developed with the material, in quiet speculation. And now, faced with the strange and insistently precise twists and turns of the material, you can follow the sequences of forces and lines and listen to thinking going on.

ADDRESS 9., Berggasse 19 [32 M 11]
CLIENT Sigmund Freud Society
ENGINEER H Locher/ K H Wagner
SIZE 4.35 square metres in lightwell, 5.27 square metres in apartment, 3.25 square metres excavated wall space
COST approximately ös 1.5 million
GETTING THERE U2 to Schottentor, then tram 37, 38, 40, 41 or 42 to Schwarzspanierstrasse
ACCESS by special request only

Additions Wolfgang Tschapeller 1991

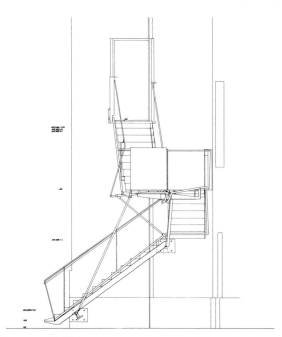

Additions Wolfgang Tschapeller 1991

Inner City

Stein's Diner

There is a certain self-conscious muted elegance to the Eichinger oder Knechtl atmospheres, a deceptively simple architectural ambience where you don't necessarily notice the concrete surface until it goes 'clunk' under your glass, you don't begin to wonder where the light actually comes from until your third or fourth visit. In the Diner light always appears from behind some other material. A shimmer which is definitively not daylight is reflected off the wooden louvres covering the windows to the street, the waved ceiling is lit from somewhere behind a mirror. There is a tension between the different surfaces – functional, material, lit/unlit, used/unused – stronger down here than in the rest of the Café Stein which is also by the same architects. There are low rows of mirrors just above the red leather benches, so only when you sit down does the space widen out – as if this city really has an underground life.

ADDRESS 9., Währingerstrasse 6/Kolinggasse [32 N 11]
CLIENT Ossi Schellman
GETTING THERE U2 or tram 1, 2 or D to Schottentor
ACCESS open

Inner City

Eichinger oder Knechtl 1993

Eichinger oder Knechtl 1993

Schullin-Uhren

All the requisites of a shop selling very small very expensive items, in this case watches, are neatly tucked into a left-over corner of Adolf Loos' 1911 house on the Michaelerplatz. The site in that famous building offers a shopfront to the very exclusive Kohlmarkt, and all the public attention which come with operating under the loaded roof of the Loos-Haus. Piva, in his own Italian way, does the situation justice. Solid pieces of thick stainless steel, black lacquer, red steel plate, curved glass. Plugged floorboards. Stainless steel skirtings and door frames. The materials are top quality, the execution is immaculate. The shop was built in two months, with Piva's brother as the main contractor. It is fitted cleverly into a corner left over from the last ground floor reorganisation, and only consists of what you can see from the door. Immediately to your left is a wall full of small cupboards for empty watch-boxes. The watches themselves are either on display behind the solid steel doors and plate glass of the shop window, or tucked away in a safe under the small curved stairs. The stairs lead up to a small mezzanine, the workshop of an English watchmaker. The watches can be handled at a small steel table in the corner and then finally bought on the leather decking of the main counter. Don't worry about the prices – the interior fully justifies your extravagant purchase.

(Paolo Piva has also designed the new extensions to Adolf Loos' Knize-shop on Graben.)

ADDRESS 1., Kohlmarkt 18 [32 N 12]
CLIENT Schullin & Söhne
SIZE 53 square metres
OTHER Adolf Loos Prize for Architecture 1994
GETTING THERE U1 or U3 to Stephansplatz or tram 1, 2, D or J to Burgring
ACCESS open

Paolo Piva 1993

Paolo Piva 1993

Kunsthistorisches Museum Café

This would be a marvellous place if it could be a regular café, if you didn't have to buy a museum ticket and if it wasn't run by one of the most expensive *Konditorien* in Vienna and populated almost exclusively by tourists. The surroundings are of course splendid, and the idea of having a café which is simply a loose arrangement of modern furniture set out in the stupendously rich upper hall of the museum, a living room suddenly appearing in the imperial halls, is very attractive.

When you sit down you are just too low to look out across the gardens of Maria-Theresien-platz; instead you come face to face with the new chairs, 10 mm bent laminate, thin and immaterial, only marred by the unfortunate choice of upholstery which is anyway quickly covered up by the backside of a grateful tourist. There are new light fittings, gleaming chrome trusses strung out out into the old space. The pastry counter is a black lifeboat of simplicity on the tidal wave of 19th-century opulence.

ADDRESS 1., 1st floor, Kunsthistorisches Museum, Maria-Theresien-Platz [32 0 11]
ORIGINAL BUILDING Gottfried Semper and Karl von Hasenauer, 1891
GETTING THERE U2 to Babenbergerstrasse or trams 1, 2, D and J to Burgring
ACCESS open

Inner City

Gert M Mayr-Keber 1988

Inner City

Gert M Mayr-Keber 1988

Museumsquartier

In October 1994 Mayor Helmut Zilk publicly declared that he favoured a 'soft renovation' of the former Imperial stables in the so-called Messe-palast. This seemingly benign remark by the Stadtvater of Vienna marked the end of a long and painful road for Ortner & Ortner's competition-winning entry for the Museumsquartier, Vienna's proposed new centre for contemporary art and culture. Ortner's project did away with most of the old stables attributed to the 18th-century Austrian architect J E Fischer von Erlach, and replaced them with a complex of buildings containing a Museum of Modern Art, a Museum for the Leopold Collection, a general-purpose venue to replace the Kunsthalle, a Museum of Architecture, a Media Centre, a Children's Museum and – last but not least – the controversial Leseturm, a 56-metre-high library tower for contemporary literature. In the beginning there was great optimism, but after four years filled with public controversy, media ridicule of the project and political opportunism, realisation seemed more and more unlikely. And in the middle of the storm, Ortner's architecture became a malleable indistinct building mass changing from month to month to accommodate new contents, new clients and collectors, as financial expediency dictated.

Zilk's support for the 'softer' alternative was its death knell. But in hindsight the story is interesting for what it demonstrates of the relation-ship between architecture and politics, which brings with it some familiar and uncomfortable dilemmas. How far should architecture cater to public taste? Who defines this taste? How far are the efforts of architects being reduced to political ammunition? And why do architects feel this as such a great injustice?

Following the death of the Ortner project, a wake was held at the Austrian Society for Architecture. One of the interesting issues addressed was whether there was anything in the proposed architecture itself which

Project, Laurids and Manfred Ortner 1988

Project, Laurids and Manfred Ortner 1988

could have influenced the final outcome.

Otto Kapfinger (theoretician): The Museumsquartier was conceived as a kind of Austrian Centre Pompidou. The Leseturm became a symbol, a polemic rather than an architectural thing. And when the tower fell, the project fell with it. Was the concept too inflexible?

Dieter Bogner (former director of the Musumsquartier development company): In the autumn of 1992 we discussed the possibility of starting afresh, but decided that this would mean having to develop a new concept, have a new competition and risk another 20 years of waiting. The owners, the city and the state, said: 'do it now'. But then the agreement was put off and never signed, and after four years it is all decided by the Mayor in 20 minutes. It was always about other things than the project itself.

Audience: Could Ortner have done a new project? The first was very rigid. The second was flexible but obviously too flexible. It had nothing imperative, which a majority could have stood behind and said: 'something will be lost if this is not built'. Could there have been another architecture which would have facilitated the process?

Bogner: We could have taken the Ortner project further, but both the owners at that point stood by it. So that was the decision. It was fully suitable for a museum.

Audience: It was too flexible, a part could always be taken out of it, the tower shortened …

Kapfinger: It is like the quote from Karl Musil: 'We don't want either or, we want either and or.'

Bogner: It is more interesting to ask why we did not succeed in building a lobby for the project. Leopold wanted to install the 'Austrian soul'

Project, Laurids and Manfred Ortner 1988

Project, Laurids and Manfred Ortner 1988

in the Museumsquartier with his collection of Klimt and Schiele. By now, Leopold is the Museumsquartier, and all the other things are no longer seen as necessary. There is also another Musil quote: 'It might just as well be something else'. It is an expression of insular thinking. Now there is no Museum of Modern Art, no Media Centre and no new Kunsthalle. And in that the city is missing something.

ADDRESS 1., Messeplatz [32 O 11]
ORIGINAL BUILDING J B Fischer von Erlach, 1690; J E Fischer von Erlach, 1721–23; extended 1850–54
CLIENT Museumsquartier Betriebsgesellschaft GmbH
GETTING THERE U2 or U3 to Volkstheater
ACCESS open

Project, Laurids and Manfred Ortner 1988

Inner City

Project, Laurids and Manfred Crtner 1988

Kunsthalle Wien

The Kunsthalle looks to be the only built trace of the Museumsquartier. It was first erected in the old rococo riding hall of the Messepalast as a climatically controlled internal exhibition room, then dismantled and re-erected at the end of the Karlsplatz. It was only ever meant to be a temporary building until Ortner & Ortner's plan for the Museumsquartier was built, but with the death of that project in October 1994 (see page 50), the Kunsthalle remains one of the few major venues in the city for exhibitions of contemporary art. It is a striking presence on the venerated Karlsplatz, between Olbrich's 1898 Secession building and Wagner's 1899 underground station, and it was of course surrounded by much controversy when it was erected. By now it is an accepted part of the inventory of the place, and there will probably be as many protests if it ever comes to taking it down again.

The hall itself is a simple yellow steel box with a sky-blue external steel structure and a clear internal space 54 metres long, 17.7 metres wide and 9 metres high, held off the ground by dark blue ground beams on concrete foundations. There is a smaller glazed box next to it containing offices, storage and the Kunsthalle Café. Servicing machinery is housed outside in 'real' containers. The exhibition hall is penetrated by a turquoise tubular steel girder which allows public access from the Girardipark through the building to the entrance on the other side.

Adolf Krischanitz: I don't like the construction of a building to be like this [grabs his left ear with his right hand over his head], I like structure to be in the background, an indirect influence, not this direct powerful thing.

IHA: But the effect of your buildings is strong enough to create quite a public reaction in a lot of cases? Like the Kunsthalle for example?

Adolf Krischanitz 1992

AK: Yes, but the Kunsthalle is another thing, the Kunsthalle is a box. People don't like it because they actually don't like to be confronted with what they themselves are doing: they're doing boxes. And if you show them straightforward boxes they are very angry, they want to have a box with a cupola and so on. But an exhibition space is a box – at the Kunsthistorisches Museum you have perhaps an image on the outside, but when you show people what it is and what it does they are angry. The Kunsthalle is a temporary construction, it had to be very cheap … I did everything they wanted, and it made them very angry.

ADDRESS 4., Karlsplatz, Treitlstrasse 2 [32 0 12]
ENGINEER Manfred Gmeiner
COLOUR Oscar Putz
CLIENT Stadt Wien
SIZE 950 square metres plan area
COST ÖS 29 million
GETTING THERE U1, U2 or U4 to Karlsplatz
ACCESS open

Adolf Krischanitz 1992

Adolf Krischanitz 1992

Wiener Loft©

Despite social housing being one of the mainstays of architectural activity and developments in the last ten years, very few architects even attempt to affect the way the housing industry is working. The Wiener Loft© project by design group ST/A/D is one of the few efforts to provoke a change in the habits of the industry without a loss of aesthetic or architectural quality. ST/A/D uses prefabrication and systematised building to challenge the economic equation of the housing industry – a challenge which, when you look at the homogeneity of even the housing projects produced by the most interesting architects, is long overdue. Prefabricated units, based on freight containers but modified and patented by ST/A/D, house all the basic domestic services: bathroom, electricity distribution, heating etc. This not only makes the most expensive items of housing construction much cheaper, it also allows greater freedom of choice in the construction and organisation of the surrounding spaces and makes a greater proportion of the budget available for example for larger floor areas. It is one of the few projects coming out of the housing construction boom to make a serious proposal for significant financial reorganisation, by virtue of being irresistibly cheaper than any currently used methods of construction. The intention of ST/A/D is to produce units for sale on the open market. Two prototype units were on display next to the Secession in 1993, a housing project is being built in the outskirts of Vienna and there are also plans to use the unit for construction of a large student housing scheme.

SIZE basic unit about 10 square metres
COST one-third of conventional housing construction

Inner City

Heidulf Gerngross and Robert Schwan 1993

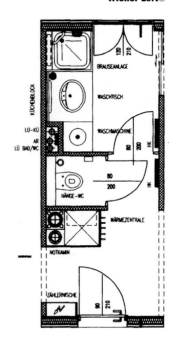

Heidulf Gerngross and Robert Schwan 1993

Stadtpark pedestrian bridge

Vienna remained a walled city longer than most other European capitals, the walls and the area around them were redeveloped into the Ringstrasse as late as the end of the 19th century. The Stadtpark is the last remainder of the Glacis, the wide belt of open land in front of the city wall which was kept open for defence purposes.

The object of the design of the new bridge was to span the river Wien with as small an elevational area as possible. The structure is simple: two steel box sections for the main arches and a flat steel girder hanging from it, all painted a vague park-green. The footway narrows towards the centre so as to give some variation to the space you are crossing, in Czech's words 'a reason for going further', before it widens out at the middle to make a place to stand and look down on the river.

ADDRESS 1., Stadtpark [32 0 12]
CLIENT Stadt Wien
COST ÖS 3 million
GETTING THERE tram 1 or 2 to
Weihburggasse and U4 to Stadtpark
ACCESS open

Inner City

Hermann Czech 1985–87

Hermann Czech 1985–87

Ringstrassen Galerien

Since its construction in the 1870s, when it replaced the old city walls the Ringstrasse has been the defining element of the city centre. The appearance of a free site in this prestigious belt is a rare occurrence.

Until recently the headquarters of car manufacturer Fiat-Steyr stood on the site. Steyr, which is also a munitions manufacturer, was discovered to have dealt arms illegally in the Iran/Iraq war and the company was more-or-less closed down. Shortly after there was a fire in the building. Only the top floors were affected, but, though it was not structurally necessary, it was decided to tear the building down.

Ringstrassen Galerien is a sparkling new development of exclusive shops and offices, housed in two new buildings linked by a steel bridge. One is the Palais Corso, a reconstruction of the façade the 19th century Palais with a steel and glass inside and a mock rococo hotel. The other is Holzbauer's Kärntnerringhof, with a simple modern exterior clearly drawn in straight lines of light stone. Inside both buildings everything gleams – polished plaster, polished brass, polished stone, chromed steel. Smooth stone cladding. Shiny like a new car.

ADDRESS 1., Kärntner Ring 5–13 [32 O 12]
ASSOCIATED ARCHITECTS Wilhelm Holzbauer with Georg Lippert (Kärntnerringhof) 1993; Neumann + Partner, Hlaweniczka + Partner and Hannes Lintl (Palais Corso) 1994
CLIENT a consortium of major Austrian banks
SIZE 18,000 square metres offices, 12,000 square metres shops and restaurants, 4000 square metres penthouse flats, 750 parking spaces, ANA Grand Hotel 205 rooms
GETTING THERE tram 1 or 2 or U1 to Oper
ACCESS open

Inner City

Wilhelm Holzbauer et al, 1993, 1994

Wilhelm Holzbauer et al, 1993, 1994

Arcadia Opera shop

The shop is set into the base of the Opera, and sells small things, from stills of rehearsals and perfomances to Opera key-rings. The thin-section hardwood and glass front carefully closes the arcades of the old building, the inside is covered with a conglomeration of small hardwood shelves. Czech's interiors are often simultaneously reassuring and disturbing: the familiarity of the materials, a red vinyl floor, veneered furniture, red and gold signs, is challenged by seemingly whimsical decisions like hanging more than 50 green glass lamps in a space of less than 150 square metres.

IHA: You have worked on a lot of existing buildings. Do you see that as a limitation?

Czech: No, because it is also a methodical question. You build up a series of decisions in a design, experience makes you select those decisions which have to be made now, and postpone others. You have a sequence of decisions in design, and you always have aspects which contradict earlier decisions. So you have the choice: you either bring them into congruence, or very often you don't and you have to skip one of them or you revise an earlier decision. The more you do this, the more your own design, before it is built, becomes a finished building which you have to remodel by further work, and the more it is not so different from working with an existing building. It might even be easier to remove parts of an existing building than to remove your own decision!

ADDRESS 1., Kärntner Strasse 40 [32 0 12]
CLIENT Erhard Löcker
SIZE 170 square metres
GETTING THERE tram 1 or 2 or U1 to Oper
ACCESS open

Inner City

Hermann Czech with Stephan Seehof 1989

Inner City

Hermann Czech with Stephan Seehof 1989

Etablissement Ronacher

The restored Ronacher is neither here nor there – most old parts have been faithfully repainted and regilt, some parts, like the ticket hall in the rotunda and the new interval bars and cloakrooms in the basement, bring an unwilling novelty into the old structure, new enough to be recognised as such but not bold enough to challenge the golden ornaments of old. In comparison, the new terrazzo floors, the fair-faced concrete, the white rotunda where Nancy Spero's delicate murals are lit by a handful of bare fluorescent tubes, the odd light fittings, the hi-tech external baldachino and sparkling moulded steel theatre seats, appear bewildered and incoherent. The architect was obviously working under the pressure of financial restrictions as well as pressure from conservationists, but so do all architects. Having got as far as he did towards a contrast between the old and the new, it is a real shame he didn't go all the way. As it is, the combination of restored old and reluctant new benefits neither.

IHA: I came across a small notice in an old magazine saying '30th of January 1991 the Mayor of Vienna, Helmut Zilk, announced that the building of Coop Himmelblau's competition-winning entry for the Ronacher Theatre will start on the 1st of April'. I knew the project from international publications of course, but I never realised it got that close to realisation. What happened?

Wolf Prix: What happened? It's easy. First, politicians are always insecure because they are always looking in the papers for the opinion polls. So they don't really decide what's going on, and they don't recognise future landmarks. And then a so-called important cultural guy moved in; he's very admired in Vienna, a very avant-garde thinker …

IHA: Who?

Prix: André Heller. He's basically a very mediocre artist but a very clever

Renovation Luigi Blau 1993

Renovation Luigi Blau 1993

Inner City

businessman. So he sells seemingly progressive and human issues in order to fill his pocket. He moved in and made a proposal so the politicians could decide the other way around: actually he killed it.

IHA: Personally?

Prix: Personally. Because he made the proposal that the theatre should be saved like it is. He will be going bankrupt very soon. So this is the basic culture.

IHA: One thing which amazes me about Vienna is that everything happens at such a personal level.

Prix: It's one of the smallest capitals of the world. There are no hierarchies, so you can see the power everywhere, which has advantages and disadvantages. People from Los Angeles always admire that we can talk to the mayor or to the city planner here if we want, but this has advantages and disadvantages at the same time, they can talk to us in the same way. But basically, it's everywhere the same, architects are on an outpost in the land of no hope.

IHA: Here.

Prix: Everywhere. No difference.

ADDRESS 1., Seilerstätte 9 [32 0 12]
CLIENT Stadt Wien
ORIGINAL BUILDING Ferdinand Fellner
NEW MURALS Nancy Spero
GETTING THERE tram 1 or 2 to Weiburggasse
ACCESS open

Renovation Luigi Blau 1993

Galerie Slavik

A machine interior. Steel cases for display of small valuable things like jewellery, small sculptures and ceramics, are hanging from a central steel beam, running the length of the room, or on tracks along the wall. The long steel beam comes out through the glass shopfront, and on the end of it sits a rotating bronze disc. The glass cases can be pushed and pulled back and forth as required, and stored at the end of the shop if not in use. Nothing touches the floor, not even the main exhibition table which is clamped on to one of the existing pillars. It is all beautifully made, but why it has to be that nothing touches the floor I am not quite sure.

ADDRESS 1., Himmelpfortgasse 17 [32 0 12]
CLIENT R and W Slavik
METALWORK Thomas Hoke
GETTING THERE tram 1 or 2 to Weiburggasse
ACCESS open

Edmund Hoke 1990

Inner City

Edmund Hoke 1990

Mozarts Sterbehaus

It was the year before the bicentenary of Mozart's death. Local media tycoon Kurt Falk, owner of *Täglich Alles*, was moved by the occasion to finance an installation marking the house where the great composer died. Ullman was at the time working with Gae Aulenti on a Mozart exhibition at the Künstlerhaus and was asked to do the installation.

Ullman: Mozart is so loaded in Vienna, through tourism and Mozartkugeln, it is almost impossible for me to listen to the music objectively … in the exhibition it was important for us to show Mozart also as an aggressive, critical person.

This collided with many people's sugared expectations. By the time the installation was built, controversy surrounded the exhibition. Claiming that it looked nothing like what he expected, Falk refused to pay the final contractors' bills, which had to be met by the City of Vienna.

The installation created an abstraction of the façade of the old house, with the help of a steel frame, a blue fabric screen and an Italian stage painter, at the point in the street where it had stood 200 years before. Another steel frame suggested the building line of the house opposite.

In February 1992 Atelier Ullmann got a call; someone had seen building work going on at the installation in Rauhensteingasse. Kurt Falk and the commemorative authorities were having the suble tones painted over with 'real' colours, 'real' windows installed with 'real' mouldings, 'real' columns either side of the door. The blue screen disappeared, the steel frame across the street was cut away.

ADDRESS 1., Rauhensteingasse 8 (now demolished) [32 0 12]
CLIENT Kurt Falk, Gemeinde Wien

Inner City

Installation Franziska Ullmann 1991–92

Inner City

Installation Franziska Ullmann 1991–92

Wahliss Passage

I first saw this small shop entrance as a second-year architecture student and was impressed by the immaculate detailing, especially after hearing teachers dismissing this kind of design as something which could never be built. Later I thought, 'only in Vienna'.

The shop entrance is a passage into the glass-covered inner courtyard containing an expensive porcelain-shop. The main element is a jagged white plane, like a shard of a broken porcelain bowl, cutting through the ceiling and poking out into the street. There is a steel version of the traditional Viennese outside display cases wrapping around the narrow shop front. Behind the glass precious items of porcelain are leaning against the rough façade of the existing building – hinting at a similarity between the glass and perspex finishes of the Himmelblau design and the white porcelain Lippizaner horses on display.

Inner City

ADDRESS 1., Kärntner Strasse 17 [32 0 12]
CLIENT Porzellanhaus Ernst Wahliss
GETTING THERE U1 or U3 to Stephansplatz
ACCESS open

Coop Himmelblau (Wolf Prix and Helmut Swiczinsky) 1986

Coop Himmelblau (Wolf Prix and Helmut Swiczinsky) 1986

American Bar (Kärntner Bar)

Turn-of the century Viennese architecture is a world-wide tourist attraction. The Secession building, Wagner's train stations, Hoffman's Postsparkasse are all as frequently photographed as the Stephansdom or the Ringstrasse. This historic self-consciousness is a very recent thing. In the early 1960s, city officials wanted to demolish buildings by Wagner, Hoffman, and Loos – it was only during the late 1960s and '70s, when work was short and most bigger commissions went to politically affiliated architects, that people like Hermann Czech, Hans Hollein, Friedrich Achleitner and others took the time to research and restore the city's architectural heritage. Kapfinger and Krischanitz restored the Werkbundsiedlung in 1983–85 and the Secession in 1985–86. This historical interest culminated in a magnificent exhibition in the Künstlerhaus in 1985, designed by Hollein and called *Vienna – Dream and Reality 1870–1930*.

The street front of Adolf Loos' American Bar was restored by Hermann Czech for *Dream and Reality* in original materials, displayed in the exhibition and later installed in the Bar itself.

IHA: Is there an identifiable architectural vision specific to Vienna?

Dietmar Steiner (director of Architktur Zentrum Wien): I think it is a question of generation. The last generation was still trying to connect to a turn-of-the-century modern thinking, they researched Wagner, Loos and Hoffman. There was a real break in thinking with the fascist period – they tried to drown every idea of modernity. During the 1930s the image of this Viennese sweetness developed, mixing elements of Biedemeier, Baroque etc. into a kind of entertainment culture for the Nazis. After the war there was really nothing – that's why the Hollein exhibition was so interesting. Architects of the 1950s, '60s and '70s were still going back to the roots of the turn of the century. Now I don't

Adolf Loos 1908, Hermann Czech 1985, Burkhardt Rukschcio 1989

know. It seems like that Viennese baggage is too strange for the young generation, somehow too strong – they are fighting against it. They grew up with the tourist culture of the '80s and they don't realise that only ten years before we had to fight to save that stuff.

IHA: Is there a continuation of tradition?

Otto Kapfinger (architect and critic): This is a very delicate thing. Of course there are continuations in thinking, in conception, in likes and dislikes. But the problem in Vienna was, and to a certain extent still is, that every architectural discussion more or less only relates to the so-called Viennese tradition. Every generation also fights the battle of the former generation, this is true, but here we still argue on Otto Wagner or Adolf Loos and on Josef Frank. This is all nice, but it is very narrow. People in Vienna think this is the middle of the world and we have it all, we had Plischke and we had Frank and the expressionism and Wagner and we can think it all out on our own. The problem I had in the '80s is that, in architectural writing as well, there are no cross-references made. And it would have been much more fruitful for the whole scene, including me, to make these crossrelations, to provoke also an architectural reflection. Because subconsciously it is there, but it is not brought out.

Inner City

ADDRESS 1., Kärntner Durchgang [32 N 12]
GETTING THERE U3 or U1 to Stephansplatz
ACCESS open

Adolf Loos 1908, Hermann Czech 1985, Burkhardt Rukschcio 1989

Adolf Loos 1908, Hermann Czech 1985, Burkhardt Rukschcio 1989

KIX bar

Oskar Putz experiments with space and colour. He has worked with many of Vienna's leading architects, but this bar is the first thing he has done on his own. The space, one big room in an existing building in the centre of the Inner City, has been skilfully divided and distorted by rectangular areas of strong colour, to the point where you do not know whether you are faced by real volumes or coloured surfaces. Toilets? They're over there, through the wall. The room resounds as your drink clanks down on the hollow steel drum table; the scale of it confuses your sense of your own comparative size. It is very high, a luxury in the Inner City where two floors of retail could have been fitted in under the ceiling.

Rather than aiding or suggesting an understanding of the space, the colour makes its own spaces across the physical. It refuses to create a sociable atmosphere, but the experts seem reluctant to blame it on the colours. Hermann Czech blamed it on the furniture, free-standing high-backed steel tube chairs and curious hollow steel tables. I took another friend there, a product designer who said: 'It's very clear. It's the floor'. This is covered with industrial aluminium plates. I think it's to do with the strictness of the overall effect: the shiny floor, the uncomfortable furniture, the undifferentiated lighting, none of which allows you to affect or change the place by your being there; it is fixed, like an exhibit, preventing you using the spaces created by those fantastic colours.

ADDRESS 1, Bäckerstrasse 4 [32 N 12]
ASSISTING ARCHITECT Kaitna
GETTING THERE U1 to Stefánsplatz
ACCESS open

Oskar Putz 1988

Oskar Putz 1988

Inner City

Wiener Hauptpost

This 18th-century secularised Benedictine monastery was restored and added to by Heinz Neumann, and Adolf Krischanitz was asked to do the Post Office hall. The development includes the Post Office, speculative offices, a small shopping mall, restaurants and cafés.

The interiors are mainly to do with light. Light is focused by lenses in big wall-mounted fittings on to polished curved steel reflectors on the ceiling, shiny shells which spread the focused light again over the white-washed walls and pale tiled floor. This somewhat over-elaborate arrangement is presumably to make use of the low vaults of the old building for maximum-intensity indirect lighting. The interior surfaces of the circulation areas are disappointingly nondescript. There is a striking contrast between the bright white light of the more general parts of the refurbishment and the filtered daylight of the former cloisters which now house the new Post Office hall. The old internal courtyard has been roofed over with a smooth multi-functional double glass skin, which incorporates air handling in ducts formed directly by the glass, and smoke ventilation by hydraulically opening panels, in addition to lighting behind the alternating clear and matt panes. This layer of operations is reflected in the sunken polished floor of the hall which brings staff up to eye level with the customers, and the only separating element is a pattern of pale green enamel on the clear glass screen, and even that is perforated – close up you have free visual access to the inner workings of the postal service.

ADDRESS 1., Fleischmarkt [32 N 12]
CLIENT Post- und Telegraphendirektion
COLOUR CONCEPT for the Post Office hall, Oskar Putz
GETTING THERE U1, U4 or tram 1, 2 or N to Schwedenplatz
ACCESS open, including a 24-hour post and telephone service

Adolf Krischanitz, Heinz Neumann 1994

Adolf Krischanitz, Heinz Neumann 1994

Falkestrasse rooftop alterations

The impressive thing about Coop Himmelblau is not their writing, not their drawings, nor their intellectual associations, all of which travel so readily around the world. The impressive thing is the way they have managed to put material together, of which there are a few examples available in Vienna. It is the connection to real structural dynamics, to the forces in the steel and the glass, which gives weight and meaning to the words, not the other way around. Which makes it doubly unfortunate that it is almost impossible get in to see the lawyers' offices on the roof in Falkestrasse, which are the best example of Coop Himmelblau's Viennese work. You get the best possible view from one of the bastions of the old city wall on Dominikanerbastei, where you can just see the end of the prestressed main truss hanging over the parapet of the old roof.

IHA: I would like to ask you about this term: 'deconstructivism'. My knowledge of it is very superficial, but it appears to me as a term which, if it hadn't contained the word 'construct', would not have fallen in the path of architects.

Wolf Prix: Take it as it was invented; it was meant as a name for a direction which is connected to the early constructivists. If you look very superficially on Tschumi's work you can say that it comes from Melnikov. Not always, but mentally, our projects are very close to the method of the French philosopher deconstructing a certain text or a poem. Therefore I don't fight this word. If someone says we are deconstructivist, yes, it could be. So for us it means that we try to find some weak points, not only in the task or the programme of the task, but also in terms of structure, and make them into very strong points. Therefore we get this floating feeling. So if we had two volumes, one big and heavy and one very small and tiny, we combine the two and support the small

Coop Himmelblau (Wolf Prix and Helmut Swiczinsky) 1988

Inner City

Coop Himmelblau (Wolf Prix and Helmut Swiczinsky) 1988

one by giving it structural meaning... and in this moment, when we combine and support the weak thing, the structure starts to float, and this makes a new aesthetic. It's very stable, it's confused sometimes with unstable things, but the image is dynamic.

IHA: What about international contacts in Viennese architecture?

Prix: This is very sad. A very very sad problem, because there are some, but you know, the Viennese are not crazy about talking to foreigners.

IHA: Rumours have it that Zaha Hadid is building here. Planning at least.

Prix: She will maybe get a commission to plan. This is the media, it's ridiculous. If someone shows up in a city they immediately say this person is building something. I heard that many times and Coop Himmelblau as well are doing buildings everywhere … it is not true!

IHA: Very few international architects have actually built something here.

Prix: Yes. Maybe we try it, but the important architects of our generation … I doubt if they can work here. Zaha of course will hopefully get it. But you know, the danger is that everyone says she is building here and everyone believes it, and then she doesn't build, but the politicians have benefited from the image that they are doing a lot of things. Therefore I'm very very angry that it is publicised before it even started. This is image-making at the expense of an architect. So: Vienna invites Zaha. I want to see the building built!

ADDRESS 1., Falkestrasse 6 [32 N 12]
CLIENT Schuppich, Sporn, Winischhofer & Schuppich
STRUCTURAL ENGINEER Oskar Graf
SIZE 400 square metres, including 90-square-metre conference room
GETTING THERE U3 or tram 1 or 2 to Stubentor
ACCESS absolutely none

Inner City

Coop Himmelblau (Wolf Prix and Helmut Swiczinsky) 1988

Coop Himmelblau (Wolf Prix and Helmut Swiczinsky) 1988

Museum für Angewandte Kunst (MAK)

For the renovation of the Museum of Applied Arts (MAK), a selection of architects and artists were invited to work with the museum curators on the display of the permanent collection of the MAK. The result is unique. When the museum reopened in 1993 it had become two superimposed museums: the first displaying the artefacts and the second displaying the displaying of the artefacts, a new collection of contemporary art created by the exhibition of the existing objects. The museum has in some cases sacrificed straight historical documentation – in the installation by Barbara Bloom, for example, the old things almost disappear in the new design. In other cases, like the rooms by Jenny Holzer or Günther Förg, a very fine balance is struck between the intentions of the artist and the meanings and values of the old things. However, what is most striking throughout is the courage of Director of the MAK, architect Peter Noever, and the curators, in choosing artists who would make strong statements of their own, and in allowing this extraordinary meeting to take place.

The permanent exhibition is divided into historical periods, one in each of nine rooms on two floors of the main museum building. In addition there is a new mezzanine loft for contemporary art, and the basement storage rooms have been opened to the public. Some are more successful than others.

Starting in the corner of the main hall, the room by Günther Förg (Romanesque/Gothic/Renaissance) takes a low-key approach. The colour blue is the only new thing challenging the set of fragile medieval vestments and heavy Renaissance majolica. The walls have been painted a strong cobalt blue, the intensity of which interrupts the placid relationship between the museum and the objects, with all the defiance of a new lover brought home to meet the family for the first time.

Passing through the Baroque/Rococo/Classicism exhibit with Donald

Renewal organised by Peter Noever, opened 1993

Renewal organised by Peter Noever, opened 1993

Judd's room within a room, back through the main hall and Franz Graf's shelves in the Renaissance/Baroque/Rococo room, where white lace is laid out on black velvet, the stitches made almost readable as a strangely crafted text, you reach the Empire/Biedermeier exhibits, arranged by Jenny Holzer. Single pieces of furniture are placed along the wall, each with a strip of electronic text above. The old pieces and the luminous band of text, writing out 19th-century documents and personal records, are set at a respectful distance to each other, both allowed to breathe. You can ignore either if you want, there is no forced juxtaposition. In contrast, the Historicism/Art Deco/Jugendstil room by Barbara Bloom is one of the most extreme, where the objects, a series of Thonet chairs, have almost been removed; there is only a shadow and a little plaque left. Bloom has lined up all the chairs behind a translucent screen and back-lit them, so their shadows form a procession through the room. All function, all materiality, all colour, all association is restricted; the chairs are mute, captured like questioned prisoners between screen and light source, sacrificed rather than brought into play in the new installation.

Upstairs you pass through the red, black, white and silver envelope of Heimo Zobernig's Wiener Werkstätte exhibition, into the display of Art Noveau/Art Deco by Eichinger oder Knechtl. Two cardboard walls, two glass boxes, one blue glass window, one long glass case. The pieces of furniture are caged in the middle of the room, their scarred backs pushed against the glass. The past has been somehow indecently exposed, the new design a smooth barrier device to protect you from contamination.

A handful of Austrian architects, Italian, Swedish and Finnish glass, a small selection of furniture, a room installation by Jasper Morrison in the middle comprises the 20th-century design and architecture exhibit by Peter Noever and Manfred Wakolbinger. This display appears surpris-

Inner City

Renewal organised by Peter Noever, opened 1993

ingly tame, despite the dynamic exhibits – perhaps because it contains only recent pieces, and in a sense gives away the game of the other rooms, without benefiting from the contrast offered by the old objects.

The Far-East Collection and basement study rooms have been made available by Lukas Schumacher's considerate design. Despite the obvious economy of materials, these rooms give a sense of privilege, as if you have been allowed to browse in your grandmother's wardrobe, and the exhibits down here are by no means less splendid than those upstairs. There are Buddhas laid out on concrete slabs, smaller objects in galvanised steel sheet and glass cases. Black tarmac on the floor, track lighting on to concrete ceilings, no attempt to be decorative. But the sheer amount of things on display allows you to choose, a welcome relief from the tight selection which has been made for you in the rest of the museum.

ADDRESS 1., Stubenring [32 N 12]
EXISTING BUILDING Heinrich von Ferstel, 1871
NEW ROOMS by Barbara Bloom, Eichinger oder Knechtl, Günther Förg and Mathis Eszterhazy, Gang Art, Franz Graf, Jenny Holzer, Donald Judd, Peter Noever, Lukas Schumacher, Hermann Strobl and Ursula Aichwalder, Manfred Wakolbinger, Heimo Zobernig
DESIGN SHOP AND BOOKSHOP Sepp Müller and Michael Embacher
STAIRCASE TOWER Sepp Müller
CAFÉ Hermann Czech
GARDEN PLATFORM Peter Noever
GARDEN GATE Walter Pichler
RING GATE James Wines, SITE
GETTING THERE U3 or tram 1 or 2 to Stubentor
ACCESS open

Renewal organised by Peter Noever, opened 1993

Inner City

Renewal organised by Peter Noever, opened 1993

MAK Café

The MAK café is another of the results of director Peter Noever's refurbishment of the Museum of Applied Arts (see page 90).

There is nothing complacent here about the relationship of new to old: the new interior fits critically into an existing room in the museum, and the undeniable quality of both makes each new detail into a commentary.

There is a big, almost circular mirror by the entrance. In this mirror you see the street you are about to leave, and yourself leaving it: you are being eyed up as you enter. The angle of the stair resists the symmetry of the existing building, cutting unsentimentally through the rustications of the old wall. The pivot of the entrance, a huge plastic eyeball lamp, is the same as those hanging above the Danube on the Reichsbrücke. Round windows open the large space of the café to the permanent exhibitions of the MAK, to medieval robes and porcelain, questioning exactly what or who is on display. Two freestanding bars face the old exhibited objects, narrow glass shelves balance on strange bundles of finely crafted broomsticks. The old painted ceiling is mirrored in the black polished glass of the tabletops. The material quality and perfect joinery reinforce the insistence of the questioning. All material joints are tight and impeccable, glass to hardwood, metal to marble, without the usual resignation of a 5-mm tolerance. Industrial aluminium lamps are suspended above, keeping the grandeur in check.

IHA: There is a quote in the presentation brochure for your new school building: 'Out of a conscious process of design comes an architecture which doesn't speak unless it's spoken to'.

Hermann Czech: Yes. It's a quote which Wolf Prix was very clever to understand: it's the old saying: 'a child should not speak unless spoken to.' [Laughs] He understood – I am also a terrible pedagogue. And I'm

Hermann Czech 1993

Kind? Weil man sich ärgert, wenn es ständig dann spricht, wenn man selber reden will. Dasselbe gilt für Architektur, sie sollte keinen Grund zur Verärgerung geben.

IHA Man könnte auch argumentieren, daß aus dem Planungsprozeß eine Architektur entsteht, aus der man die intellektuelle oder künstlerische Intention des Architekten klar herauslesen kann, und daß diese Klarheit ein Qualitätsmerkmal ist.

Czech Das ist die Ausdrucksweise des Architekten, aber die sollte einen nicht gleich wie mit einem Hammer „erschlagen". Das Problem eines bewußten Planungsprozesses und seines Ergebnisses als etwas, das nicht unbedingt wahrgenommen werden muß, stammt aus Josef Franks Theorie des Zufälligen. Er sagte, „gestaltet die Umgebung so, daß es aussieht, als sei sie zufällig so entstanden". Das Schwierige daran ist nur, wie man dies macht. Wohl nicht dadurch, daß man die Gestaltung dem Zufall überläßt. Wenn man seine Effekte nicht kontrolliert, gerät man in Auswirkungen, die man nicht vorhergesehen hat. Außerdem lachen die Leute über Dinge, von denen man das nie erwartet hätte. Also muß man seine Scherze gründlich durchdenken, man muß wissen, welche Wirkungen man erzielen möchte, und diese herausheben. So etwas lernt man aus der Erfahrung, und die Erfahrung erwirbt man beim Bauen. Es geht nicht anders. Aber jeder dieser Prozesse dauert ein bis zwei Jahre, weil ein Gebäude nun mal diese Zeit braucht, um fertig zu werden. Und deshalb ist Architektur ein Job für alte Leute. [Lacht]

Man kommt irgendwann dahin, bestimmte Dinge in einem von Czech gestalteten Raum zu erwarten, wie ein altes Familienmitglied, das nach langen Jahren in der Fremde zu Besuch kommt.

ADRESSE   1., Museum für Angewandte Kunst, Stubenring 5 [32 N 12]
GRÖSSE   500 m²
ANFAHRT   U3 oder Straßenbahn Linien 1 oder 2 bis Stubentor
ZUTRITT   frei, montags Ruhetag

Hermann Czech 1993

Innenstadt

Hermann Czech 1993

U-bahn

Vienna has an excellent public transport system. You can get from the centre to almost anywhere within the city's 23 districts in less than half an hour, and you rarely have to walk more than ten minutes from any bus-, tram- or underground station. The sign systems are impeccable, even the smallest bus stop clearly named as well as announced in advance. Public expectations are high, and with more and more areas being developed on the periphery, easy access to the centre is taken for granted. This wide coverage is achieved by a combination of low-speed surface travel (trams and buses), and high-speed underground travel: the U-bahn.

The design of the U-bahn is the work of a team of architects who won the first competition in 1971, and they have been doing it ever since. Limiting the job to one group of designers over more than 20 years means, of course, that they have the chance to become very familiar with their task, and Architektengruppe U-bahn have also designed, for example, the underground system in Vancouver.

One of the first design decisions was to create an image for the overall system rather than for each station. This has resulted in a sleek industrial design applied with few but interesting variations throughout the city. The stations are divided into safe and dangerous areas: white, bright and smooth platforms and corridors, dark and rough tracks. Lifts and entrance pavilions are open or glazed as much as possible for overview and security. Each line is identified by a colour, the sizes of the coloured surfaces depending on the velocity of travel: large where a train speeds past, small in the pedestrian areas, keeping the overall effect neutral and unified.

On its way through the city the modular construction system has been adapted to cope with archaeological excavations, open as well as closed stations, overground as well as underground tracks, resulting in a variety

Architektengruppe U-bahn 1970–94

Inner City

Architektengruppe U-bahn 1970–94

of solutions which, despite their neutral appearance, identify quite precisely the differences of each situation.

The latest additions have been to the U3, first three new stations underneath the refurbished Mariahilferstrasse, and now Schweglerstrasse and Johnstrasse stations, opened in September 1994, extending the U3 out to the large new shopping complex and housing development being built at the Meislmarkt. The continuing extension of the U-bahn net has been criticised: it is very expensive both to install and operate compared to surface-running systems. However, according to Hannes Swoboda, City Councillor for Planning and Transport, the U-bahn is the only thing which will keep people from using their cars. Tram and bus do not have the same public appeal. Speed is of course important in tying the developing areas to the north and south of the city to the centre, but it is also a question of image, making the U-bahn the only really effective tool in large-scale city planning.

ARCHITEKTENGRUPPE U-BAHN Wilhelm Holzbauer, Heinz Marschalek and Georg Ladstätter, Bert Gantar
CLIENT Stadt Wien-Wiener Stadtwerke Verkehrsbetriebe
SIZE 47 km of track and 65 stations in 1994
COST ÖS 60 billion up to September 1994

Architektengruppe U-bahn 1970–94

Architektengruppe U-bahn 1970–94

Margareten to Josefstadt

Zentagasse

The individual housing units of this corner block are protected from the noise of the street by a wall of glazed access galleries. The glass is textured and appears translucent from the street. Nothing spectacular is made of it, no fancy lighting, just strip lights which come on when someone is in the corridor, as in every other housing scheme, and no artistry with murals, the wall behind is painted a uniform bright red. The uneven spacing of the glazing bars is just enough to bring it away from the simply schematic.

The back of the building is plain, rendered, with an even grid of full-height double windows giving maximum daylight to the single-aspect flats looking out to a little communal garden. On the front there are only the solid doors of the flats facing the glass galleries. Every now and then a hazy figure maneuvres a pram over to the lift, or someone disappears into a flat – the whole thing has a simple utilitarian feel, it remains rooted in a social and material reality, unseduced by its own fashion potential.

ADDRESS 5., Zentagasse 46/Margareten-
strasse 89 [44 Q 11]
CLIENT Gemeinde Wien
USER PARTICIPATION PLANS Eduard Ebner
ENGINEER Hejkrlik
SIZE 30 units average 61 square metres,
three shops, 23 parking spaces
GETTING THERE U4 to Pilgramgasse or bus
59A to Margaretenplatz
ACCESS none

G Lautner, P Scheifinger, R Szedenik, C Schindler 1994

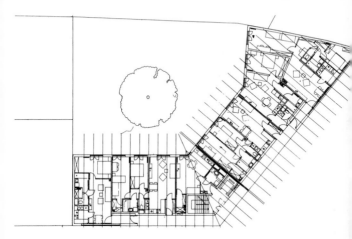

G Lautner, P Scheifinger, R Szedenik, C Schindler 1994

Viktor-Christ-Gasse

The restriction imposed by the only constructional option left for social housing – concrete frame, thermal brick infill, render – offers nothing in terms of material definition and tends to homogenise most contemporary housing projects. But not in this case. A huge, darkly pink curve with deep-set windows turns a corner in a district of old four-storey perimeter block-housing, swinging again before the junction with the next building to avoid a tree. All credit to the architect for convincing the city authorities that it was worth sacrificing potential floor area to try out other possibilities. The street line is kept by a two-storey concrete pergola, and the curve is clearly drawn against the sky by a wide white overhang at the top.

The flats were developed with a limited form of user participation. The only fixed item in the layout of was the positioning of the bedrooms to the back, otherwise the incoming inhabitants were free to choose from a wide variety of different living room/kitchen solutions. The flats also incorporate possibilities for dividing off another bedroom.

The six floors squeezed into the same height as the surrounding four affects the scale of the building, makes it appear bigger, and at the same time it increases expectations: the limited effect of the curve at street level is a slight disappointment; it is too close to the pergola to create a useable intermediate space and remains somewhat of a schematic gesture.

ADDRESS 5., Victor-Christ-Gasse 15–17/Zentagasse 35 [44 Q 11]
CLIENT Gemeinde Wien
ENGINEERS Stefan Novotny & Wolfgang Bauer
SIZE 31 units, average 66 square metres, dental surgery, 35 parking spaces
GETTING THERE U4 to Pilgramgasse or tram 62 or 65 to Laurenzgasse
ACCESS none

G Lautner, P Scheifinger, R Szedenik, C Schindler 1991

G Lautner, P Scheifinger, R Szedenik, C Schindler 1991

Mariahilfer Strasse 123

The renovation of Mariahilfer Strasse was completed in 1993. The u-bahn running underneath it, the U3, has had two new stations added to it: the stage has been set for commercial development. The new speculative office building at the end of the street has all the predictable attractions of rentability: the dynamic of modern business reflected in aluminium panels and clip-fastened horizontal strip windows, and an added expensive touch in strategic places like red stone cladding marking the double-height entrance and beechwood handrails in the staircase.

However those materials stop as soon as you have been enticed through the door. Inside there is white emulsion and terrazzo tile like any public housing project, with little architectural interest to detract from the obvious economising. No view from or light to the staircase, little sense of spatial sequence or orientation. A standard white steel frame atrium covers the shop at first-floor level. The rental office floors have a nice view out to an open part of the city centre, but nothing of its own to leave any strong impression. The two-storey base is pulled in behind a row of columns which makes the building sit rather uncomfortably on the site; add to that the receding hairline of the inclined top floors and the building begins to make a rather apologetic impression. It is nicely put together but little care seems to have gone into the planning, which is disappointing from someone like Neumann who has the experience and the organisation to pull off much better things.

ADDRESS 6., Mariahilfer Strasse 123 [31 P 10]
CLIENT Bygg & Fast
GETTING THERE U3 or U6 to Westbahnhof
ACCESS open

Heinz Neumann 1994

Heinz Neumann 1994

Skala Bar-Restaurant

Like other recent cafés, and not only in Vienna, the Skala is all about the materials. But here there is a lot more going on than a poised tension between plywood and plastic: this place is active and preoccupied with its own things, to which you as a visitor are incidental and largely unimportant. You can watch it operate if you wish, then again if you don't it doesn't much matter.

The ceiling and floor in the bar are shiny black. In the middle of the array of tables there are two sheets of black glass and a small machine emitting a beam of red light which bounces back and forth between them. There is an aquarium with moving plastic fish in the wall between the toilet lobby and the café. There is a large mirror on the old brick pier in the middle of the main room, with a steel screen held at arm's length in front of it. There are, apparently, films being projected from the toilet onto the wall of the little outside patio, there are one-way mirrors.

At first all this seems like an affront; as a guest you are accustomed to being the centre of attention, but after a while all these inexplicable things become familiar, a landscape of benign events which diverts the public attention and leaves you in undisturbed privacy to do whatever you wish to do in a café.

ADDRESS 7., Neubaugasse 8 [32 0 11]
CLIENT Gastronomiebetrieb & Kulturveranstaltungs GmbH
SIZE 250 square metres
GETTING THERE U3 to Neubaugasse
ACCESS open

Georg Driendl and Gerhard Steixner 1988

Georg Driendl and Gerhard Steixner 1988

Stadthalle Hall E

The main Stadthalle, an aluminium-clad concrete and steel structure spanning 100 metres, was finished by Roland Rainer in 1958 after an international competition. The baths next to it, also by Rainer, were completed in 1970, and the new Hall E is the most recent addition.

At 85, in a time when everything is possible, Rainer is still a refreshingly hard-boiled modernist. He knows what is good and what is bad. Every decision in the Stadthalle has its logical reason within the overriding concerns of economy and flexibility. The old Stadthalle achieves this by a modesty of materials and ingenious technical solutions. The purposely sagging roof minimises serviceable air volume, improves the reflection of sound without impeding sightlines and is stable enough to hold lighting rigs without shaking. The impressive steel structure and exposed services of the baths are an object-lesson in the architecture of baring it all.

Hall E, an independent multi-purpose space located between the big hall and the baths, follows the same unfaltering lines: mimimun means and maximum flexibility. A white steel solid-web truss construction with a free span of 25 metres, two walls perforated brick and two walls fully glazed. The services run in the ceiling through the web of the trusses. Through the 1958 foyer you see the gleaming new vent shafts of the underground carpark, providing an external focus which even manages to give the old hall back some of its intended transparency.

ADDRESS 15., Vogelweidplatz, Märzstrasse, Gablenzgasse [311 O 10]
CLIENT Wiener Stadthallen Betriebsgesellschaft
STRUCTURAL ENGINEER Albert P Raunicher
SIZE new hall 1250 square metres
GETTING THERE U6 or tram 6 or 18 to Burggasse-Stadthalle
ACCESS open

Margareten to Josefstadt

Roland Rainer 1994

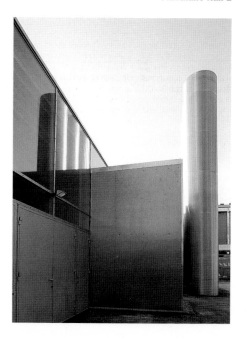

Margareten to Josefstadt

Roland Rainer 1994

Wiberg shop

Clear, simple elements and minimal detailing makes the most of a very limited space for a clothes shop. The full-height glass door is protected at night by a full-height sheet of wood, the shop front is a simple piece of plate glass set into plain concrete. Inside a precisely proportioned wooden mezzanine fills the little space, clever positioning of mirrors extends the room underneath it where the ceiling slopes back into a minimalist grotto.

Margareten to Josefstadt

ADDRESS 8., Josefstädterstrasse 70 [31 N 10]
CLIENTS Judith Widecki and Susanna Bergmann
SIZE 62 square metres
OTHER shortlisted for the Adolf Loos Prize for Architecture 1994
GETTING THERE tram J or 5 to Albertgasse
ACCESS open

Atelier Pichelman 1992

Atelier Pichelman 1992

Die Erste Bank branch office

The site was a disused cinema, the Albert-kino. The new contents cleverly make use of all the elements of the past function – the entrance loggia, open to the street in summer, the ticket hall, and the gallery – carrying on the new life of the city in the rooms of the old.

The materials are signals of new inhabitation. Primary loadbearing members are left in fair-faced concrete, secondary ones painted blue, spatial dividing elements are in red laminate, major functional pieces are veneered plywood. The space is defined by the tension between these signals and the sequence in which they are discovered. On the ground floor the long red laminate counter divides customers from staff; above the entrance the same material separates the manager from the rest of the office spaces. From a small balcony he or she can survey the entire interior. The same silky veneer forms tables and benches for the customer, the balustrade of the office gallery and the large wall at the end of the room, which penetrates down to the basement vaults and hides the concrete staircase. The whole is simple, graphic, clearly organised and finished with a precision made possible and enhanced by industrial materials.

The external façade does not conform to the interior codes. It is clad in simple aluminium strip elements, with little anodised golden coins as spacers: it wraps the corner in aluminium, like a safe, and speaks to the city of the pleasure of being a bank.

ADDRESS 8., Josefstädter Strasse 75 [31 N 10]
CLIENT Erste Österreichische Spar-Casse Bank
ENGINEER Büro Vasco
COST ÖS 15.6 million
GETTING THERE tram J or 5 to Albertgasse
ACCESS open

Boris Podrecca 1993

Margareten to Josefstadt

Boris Podrecca 1993

Restaurant Kiang II

It is difficult not to compare the second Kiang to the first (see page 28): the new restaurant does not have the material mystique of the first, it is smoother, but more open and more comfortable.

The front façade is of black glass, precisely framed in aluminium. You enter through a frosted glass door. The granite and blue laminate bar has a clear view of the entire room through a mirror-dressed cut-out in the wall behind. A long bench stretches the entire width of the room. Tall french doors give out onto a little patio at the back. Light comes from behind the white suspended ceiling and from fittings hidden in recesses behind the long bench. Everything is clear, clean and generously dimensioned. The problems and the solutions are all visible and elegantly dealt with, but without the intriguing choices and tensions of the by now old restaurant in the first district.

ADDRESS 8., Lederergasse 14 [31 N 10]
FABRIC DESIGN Doris Evdokimidou
GETTING THERE tram 43 or 44 to Skodagasse or tram 5 to Florianigasse
ACCESS open

Silvia Fracaro and Alexander Fitzek 1991

Margareten to Josefstadt

Silvia Fracaro and Alexander Fitzek 1991

Landstrasse to Simmering

Bank Austria Customer Centre

Bank Austria uses modern architecture to establish its public profile – newspaper coverage of the bank invariably includes a picture of the new customer centre in the 3rd district. It is constructed around the skeleton of a 1965 steel-frame building by Artur Perotti, one of the first projects Domenig worked on after leaving school. The old steel frame had to be completely stripped down to remove the asbestos linings. In its place stands a refurbishment which is more a luxury club for banking than your local branch office: leather furniture, Persian rugs, three TV channels to watch while you are waiting, including MTV and American financial news. No expense has been spared in the choice of materials: polished plaster and granite inside, the façade glass wrapped in a fine mesh of stainless steel sunscreens.

The bank is intended to be used for exhibitions and other cultural arrangements, for which the atrium was opened and the glass and water podium installed at the bottom of the sculptural red concrete staircase with a separate 'cultural entrance'. In the corner of the atrium is a 'green tower', a steel frame carrying 48 shiny planting pods with plants specially selected from the gardens of the Schönbrunn Palace, watered by a system of tubes hanging underneath. Ecology was also part of the concept of customer-friendliness – solvent-free paints, breathing emulsion, plasterboard as humidity-regulator, low-formaldehyde chipboard, granite checked for acceptable levels of gamma rays and radon emission.

ADDRESS 3., Vordere Zollamtsstrasse 13 [33 O 13]
CLIENT Bank Austria
GETTING THERE among others U3 or U4, and tram O to Wien Mitte
ACCESS open

Artur Perotti 1965, renovation Günther Domenig 1992

Artur Perotti 1965, renovation Günther Domenig 1992

Hundertwasserhaus

Hundertwasser is rapidly becoming as much of a tourist attraction in Vienna as Gustav Klimt, and the new Experience-Shopping Centre next to the Hundertwasserhaus indicates that Professor Hundertwasser is more than willing to capitalise on the hoardes of people who come to admire his painted façade.

I don't mind a decorated house. The colours are nice. What I do mind is the deception: behind the proclaimed ecological radicalism of colours and greenery, Hundertwasser has done nothing new. The construction is concrete frame and rendered blockwork like any other housing project. The plans are clumsy. There is nothing to learn, no technical, constructional or architectonic inventions, not even on the level of ecological building which the artist claims as one of his main inspirations.

There are other examples of bad architecture in Vienna. What makes this particular one irritating is that the unchallenged media attention gives it a seal of approval as part of the architectural development of a city which really knows better.

Hundertwasser's remedial suggestions ('Once you make the windows dance by designing each one differently, you give the building a chance to recover') are limited to the surface, but presented with all the fervour of a 19th-century quack flogging his bottles of coloured horsepiss as a miracle cure for all diseases.

ADDRESS 3., Löwengasse 41–43 [33 O 13]
CLIENT Gemeinde Wien
SIZE 52 units of 30–128 square metres, 1000-square-metre roof terrace
COST ÖS 80 million
GETTING THERE tram N to Löwengasse
ACCESS to souvenir shop

Friedensreich Hundertwasser 1985

Friedensreich Hundertwasser 1985

Offices Barichgasse

Though Vienna is developing rapidly on green-field sites in the suburbs, there are also many examples of very successful inner city infill, like this office building on a quiet residential street in the 3rd district.

One of the problems with inner city office developments is of course the need for parking, which tends to prevent the building from contributing much to the street at ground level. This is quite elegantly solved here by making the pedestrian entrance the axis of a very symmetrical little forecourt, slightly pulled back from the street line, framed by car entrances on either side where you see through into the big internal courtyard behind. The entrance to the underground car park is in the courtyard, so there is no need for descending ramps and roller shutters on the street. The central axis of the façade is emphasised by a six-storey violet column. A little ceremonial perhaps, but the insistent symmetry is more than made up for by the layers of fine steelwork in windows and balconies and the thorough and elegant detailing.

ADDRESS 3., Barichgasse 38–42/Ungargasse 59–61 [33 P 13]
ENGINEER Peter Ferro
SIZE 38: 1964 square metres, 40–42: 3385 square metres, 54 parking spaces
GETTING THERE tram O to Neulinggasse
ACCESS to court from Ungargasse

Schweger & Partner with Iwan Zdenka 1989

Kardinal-Nagl-Platz

The site for this infill housing is a gap in the perimeter block of the Rabenhof, one of the largest of Vienna's 1920s' social housing projects, an irregular agglomeration of courtyards with more than 1000 flats. The new building fits naturally into the row without making nostalgic concessions, adding a little decorative touch of its own to the surrounding romanticism with two large stainless-steel vent shafts from the underground parking running up the façade above the entrance.

The rest of the construction is the usual rendered concrete structure, and the flats, though relatively spacious, are conventionally divided into separate rooms with little flexibility of layout. All the flats have balconies or loggias, open to the south, glazed to the north. The back faces directly onto one of the courtyards of the Rabenhof, connected by a sunken semicircular courtyard. The windows to Kardinal-Nagl-Platz are small and the plain rendered façade anonymous. The main integrity of the building comes from its self-conscious symmetry which separates it clearly from the neighbouring buildings and gives it a ceremonial air of its own.

ADDRESS 3., Kardinal-Nagl-Platz 6–7 [33 P 14]
CLIENT Gemeinde Wien
SIZE 38 units, two shops, 130 parking spaces
GETTING THERE U3 to Kardinal-Nagl-Platz
ACCESS to court from St Nikolaus-Platz or Rabenweg; none to building

Günther Oberhofer 1994

Wohnpark Rennweg

The traditions of Viennese social housing, technical and typological, have been stretched tight as a sausage-skin around this fast-track mega-development. The massive scale of several hundred flats is legitimised by the faint memory of the super-blocks of the 1920s and '30s, but this has very little of the social symbolism or attitude of those developments.

A large perimeter block starts on the corner of Rennweg and Oberzellergasse and continues around to Landstrasser Hauptstrasse, with two storeys of shops and offices behind a double-height colonnade to the street, and five storeys above. Inside the perimeter there are more houses including five gaily coloured smaller square blocks by Nehrer & Medek which are entered from Landstrasser Hauptstrasse at first-floor level, corresponding to the level of the old church and the former military barracks on the Rennweg side. The level discrepancy allows street-level goods access and parking for the commercial spaces, but leaves the housing blocks looking down into car parks and loading bays through the openings between the ground-floor gardens. This is just one of many examples of a strategic decision which, although financially attractive, becomes very difficult to deal with at a smaller scale.

The predictable, standard subsidised flats express few clear definitions of the priorities in social housing. This is a general problem: despite the enormous amount of housing built (the city aims to build 10,000 units a year), the many regulations governing the quantities of housing construction, square metres, window area, sanitary provisions and so on, make it difficult to demonstrate any conscious attitude towards new qualities of living. One exception in this case is Anton Schweighofer who has managed quite successfully to implement his ideal plan of equal spaces which can be inhabited in a number of different ways, allowing an essential quality of modern life: choice.

Architektengruppe Rennweg 1994

Architektengruppe Rennweg 1994

The external appearance of the buildings is homogenised by the method of construction, in-situ concrete frames and rendered insulation. The climate in Vienna allows outer walls to be constructed with a single skin of thermal blockwork which is covered with hard fibre or extruded polystyrene insulation batts. Render is applied directly to the insulation – and that's that. Even the free-standing elements, external columns and beams, have to be covered by polystyrene to avoid cold bridges. The ideal of this kind of sleeping-bag construction is really a building with no openings, or even better, no building at all.

The lack of any visible social symbolism means that the new developments, while feeding on the memory of the old super-blocks for their profitable scale, do not have the power of those projects to create associations and memories of their own. Financial expediency has stretched it all too thin, there are too many standard solutions, it contributes nothing very memorable apart from its size. The Viennese are extremely tolerant towards new housing, they complain and they criticise, but eventually they move in with their garden furniture, and we will see …

ADDRESS 3., Landstrasser Hauptstrasse 148 [33 P 13/14]
ARCHITECTS Architektengruppe Rennweg: Atelier 4; Bramhas, Waclawek & Karrer; Marschalek & Ladstätter with Bert Gantar; Nehrer & Medek; Neumann & Steiner; Perotti & Greifeneder; Puchhammer & Wawrik; Roland Rainer; Udo Schrittwieser; Anton Schweighofer
ENGINEER Fuld and Stella & Stengel
CLIENT WEVAG
SIZE 437 flats, shops and offices, 627 parking spaces
GETTING THERE tram 71 to Landstrasser Hauptstrasse
ACCESS to grounds

Architektengruppe Rennweg 1994

Architektengruppe Rennweg 1994

Rosa Jochmann-Schule

In a programme as ambitious as that for housing, Vienna is injecting over Ös 7 billion into more than 30 new schools – the so-called 'Schulbauprogramm 2000'. Building schools has great political and social symbolism, which makes it even more significant that the schools are being very consciously used to promote good architecture. This is not least due to City Councillor Hannes Swoboda, who speaks of school building as 'architectonic research into the future'. Some of the first commissions of the Schulbauprogramm were given to the architects who represented Austria at the 1991 Venice Biennale. Peichl, Holzbauer, Hollein, Czech, Richter, Prochazka, Lainer/Auer, most have built or are building schools. Two practices not commissioned so far are Eichinger oder Knechtl and Coop Himmelblau: neither is a member of the Architects' Chamber. Hopefully, the city officials' commitment to quality will be able to cut through the professional bureaucracy.

Czech's school is built on a beautiful site in the 11th district, at the edge of an old riverbed which is now part of a wide industrial landscape. The building lies at the end of a sloping road between old five-storey perimeter-block apartment houses. As soon as you enter the main hall you see the industrial stretch beyond, the four domed brick cylinders of the gasometers, a landmark on the way in from Swechat Airport. The school is an irregular arrangement of two- to three-storey blocks, minimising the necessary length of corridor and maximising use of the oddly-shaped site. The blocks are all at angles to each other, forming internal courts and always turning the view to the outside back on to another part of the building. This allows you to orientate yourself, not by the abstract understanding of a plan diagram, but through the repeated experience of the unique landscape of the building. Standard solutions are applied throughout. Standard windows, finishes, classroom sizes, nothing chal-

Hermann Czech with Wolfgang Reder 1994

Hermann Czech with Wolfgang Reder 1994

lenges the expectations of the school-building norms. Nothing? Nothing and everything – despite the seeming resignation to traditional expectations, there is nothing obvious in the assembly of solutions. On the contrary, the result appears more critical, more precise, through the visible and conscious choices made in how the standard elements are used.

IHA: What were the schools like before the Schulbauprogramm?

Hermann Czech: Naja ... I'm not a pedagogue. I had no idea what a school should look like, because you would have to think about education, all of it, and to make a classroom open on two or three or more sides is not subversive, it's only maybe irritating or destructive to the things the teachers want to do. Why do little children have to be educated in a closed room at all? In Islamic architecture they are not, they are in an open arcade where they run around, or children in a farmyard, they learn where they are and see things. There is also a reason for the concentrated acoustically sealed atmosphere, but I don't think this has to be all day for small children. But you won't change that by architecture. So why not give the teachers what they want? In any case children are better educated today than before. You have already had a more open and less neurotic education than I had. There has been some progress, but most of this progress is in terms of the content of the education, not the shape of the rooms.

ADDRESS 11., Fuchsröhrenstrasse 21–25 [45 Q 14]
SIZE 19 classes, Volksschule
COST ÖS 116 million
GETTING THERE tram 71 from Schwarzenbergplatz to Geystrasse
ACCESS by appointment

Hermann Czech with Wolfgang Reder 1994

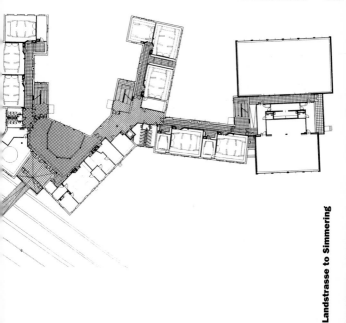

Landstrasse to Simmering

Hermann Czech with Wolfgang Reder 1994

XXX Gazometer

As part of Eichinger oder Knechtl's city-planning strategy for Vienna, Gregor Eichinger organises raves.

IHA: I can imagine that you avoid the frustration that many architects have: if they can't sit at a drawing board and be an architect, they think something is wrong and feel tragic and hard done by.

Eichinger: We do city planning by Techno-parties. It's only music, and there's a room, and people, and a huge light x into the air. It is the biggest party in Austria, as far as I know Techno-parties. The place is also very big.

IHA: Why the gasometers?

Eichinger: Because it is such a big space, but it is also so interesting because of the floor topography, which is a concrete hill. The Big Wheel in the Prater fits inside the gasometer completely. It's huge, it's like indoor open air. But the problem is you have 16 times echo in it, so only Techno is possible. And it was fun, because we started the first Gazometer three years ago; the Techno scene was just starting in Vienna, we are the barometer of the Techno scene. It is our city-planning contribution.

ADDRESS 11., Gasometer Guglgasse [46 Q 15]
CLIENT XXX Holding
SIZE 60 metres diameter, 60 metres high
GETTING THERE U3 to Schlachthausgasse, then bus 78A or 79A to Kappgasse (if they still run at midnight)
ACCESS subject to security search

Landstrasse to Simmering

J Bauer and G Eichinger 15 October 1994

J Bauer and G Eichinger 15 October 1994

Ernst-Happel-Stadion

The first stadium (1931) was an open fair-faced in-situ concrete construction. Where the impressive rough concrete structure has not been obscured by later additions you can see right through to the inside, to the seats on the other side of the bowl.

The new roof extends the original concrete skeleton with a self-supporting light steel structure. An enormous white ring-beam is placed carefully on the existing columns, and a system of struts and wires carries a roof which is suspended inside the bowl, invisible from outside. The patented Frantl-method allows you to add gradually and avoid unequal loads on the old structure: the new frame is made by stretching wires across, outlining the entire structural grid to come, then fastening the proper structural members to the wires and finally welding them together to form a self-supporting structure strong enough to carry the internal roof.

The new white steel top has a structural clarity and logic which elegantly bypasses the clumsy additions of the 1950s and seems a natural extension of the first concrete skeleton.

ADDRESS 2., Meiereistrasse 7 [34 N/O 15]
CLIENT Wiener Stadthalle – KIBA
ORIGINAL BUILDING Erich Otto Schweitzer, 1931; extensions by Theodor Schöll, 1959
ENGINEERS Willibald Zemler and Albert P Raunicher
SIZE 52,000 seats
GETTING THERE U1 to Praterstern, then tram 21 to Stadion
ACCESS open

New roof Erich Frantl, Peter Hofstätter, Robert Sturmberger 1986

Landstrasse to Simmering

New roof Erich Frantl, Peter Hofstätter, Robert Sturmberger 1986

Neue Welt Schule

Adolf Krischanitz has built a black concrete Kindergarten in the Prater for the children of Jewish emigrees. At first I thought it was a bad joke.

IHA: It seems problematic to choose a black house for a Kindergarten.
Krischanitz: Yes.
IHA: You don't have a problem with that?
Krischanitz: No. I couldn't imagine having white render on the outside, but I also couldn't imagine coloured render. Children don't think in our categories. We try to say children have to live in multi-coloured rooms, because it makes them happy. I don't believe that. I have been wanting to build a black house, but so far it was impossible. And then Federle said 'OK, we do it black, what's the problem?' It was the scandal of Vienna, like the Kunsthalle, but I like scandals. So now it's black, and everybody says 'Well, it's not so bad'. It's a question of seeing it and living in it. The black colour is a very soft stucco which reflects the green of the Prater; it looks like an old tree. Then you have the green glass panels with the sharp mirror-effect, so you have the soft mirror of the stucco and the sharp mirrors of the glass. For me it was really interesting to do a black house.

ADDRESS 2., Aspernallee/Schwartzenstockallee [34 P 16]
CLIENT Neue Welt fond
COLOUR Helmut Federle
COST ÖS 15 million
GETTING THERE U3 to Schlachthausgasse, then bus 77A to Lusthaus
ACCESS to grounds

Adolf Krischanitz 1994

Landstrasse to Simmering

Landstrasse to Simmering

Adolf Krischanitz 1994

Schmidgunstgasse

The almost impossible density of this housing project could not have been achieved had it not been for the great precision with which the few simple repeated elements of the main unit, a two-storey, four-bedroom house, have been employed. The irregularly shaped site disrupts any ideal layout and makes a dense warren of narrow pathways and twisting hedged alleys betwen the rows of houses. But unlike many similar housing projects where two rows of fronts form a street, here the front of one row faces the back of the other. This sudden proximity of public front to private back poses a delicate problem which is sensitively solved by the windows on the front opposite: minimal openings on ground floor and angled bays above avoid overlooking. Social interaction takes place as an incidental result of individual routines, through choice, rather than explicit arrangement. This non-hierarchical social approach shapes the overall plan which has no artificially constructed centre, no piazza with a little fountain or an empty common room.

In contrast to for example the narrow-fronted houses of the typical English terrace, the wide front allows you to enter right into the spatially and functionally open middle of the plan rather than at one end of a narrow corridor, you can separate the staircase from the living spaces and ascend undisturbed, and you easily get light from both sides.

ADDRESS 11., Schmidgunstgasse 61 [46 S 15]
CLIENT GSG
SIZE 61 units
GETTING THERE tram 71 or 72 to Zentralfriedhof 3. Tor, then bus 72A to Zinnergasse
ACCESS to grounds

Franz E Kneissl 1991

Franz E Kneissl 1991

Favoriten to Inzersdorf

School Pernerstorferstrasse

It's all very straightforward and very effective. The extension of Jagdgasse cuts right through the school to the tram depot on the other side, dividing it into two halves with an open public throughway down the middle. Spanning this throughway, a fully glazed steel-frame assembly hall at first-floor level makes a covered outside entrance area between the two new blocks. From the hall itself you have a wide view out into the neighbourhood on both sides, south down Jagdgasse and north over the tram stalls.

All the main strategic decisions tie the school to its location: the street, the trams, the outdoor sportsground which is set deep in the back courtyard, the Hof, the surrounding old apartment buildings. It ties into what is most inner-city children's home environment anyway, but by giving it a new use it gives the possibility of new associations to both school and home. It adds another meaning, another possible dimension to the familiar: a good definition of learning.

ADDRESS 10., Pernerstorferstrasse 43–45/Jagdgasse 22–23 [44 R 12]
CLIENT Stadt Wien
SIZE 12 + 8 classes, Volksschule
GETTING THERE U1 to Reumannplatz or tram O or 6 to Quellenplatz
ACCESS by appointment

Manfred Nehrer and Reinhard Medek 1993

Manfred Nehrer and Reinhard Medek 1993

School Absberggasse

'Paradise is exactly where we are.'

The plan is simple. The broad front of a red horizontal block faces a 1960s' housing development across a sports ground, a pond and a park. This long block contains common rooms and facilities, has the gymnasia at one end and administration and special rooms at the other. The classrooms are housed in perpendicular blocks at the back. But simplicity ends there. This uncomplicated diagram has been pulled and pushed, squeezed and turned as it developed in detail, until the most striking thing about the finished building is the multitude of differences coexisting within it. There is green glass, rubber, plywood and deep ultramarine render, strip lighting on industrial cable trays and fine stainless steel. The obvious economy in the choice of materials does not prevent refinement of execution. The toilets are different from the classroom lockers which are different from the staircase – not in the post-modern way of a collage of unrelated associations; here the differences come from each element acknowledging its specific and unique place in the whole, its function, its construction, its orientation. You might think this rather obvious, but in an architectural world where the orthogonal grid is still a primary agent of understanding, design is more often than not a process of resolving rather than emphasising life's inevitable contradictions.

The result is a building with more room than many others having more floor area – the meeting of seemingly incongruous forms creates spaces, corners, niches, where activity is not predicted, where there is room for children and young people, where there are no preconceptions of what children would 'like'. Only bad teachers can spoil this now.

Rüdiger Lainer: For me the social implementation of architecture is very important. I don't think that you can really change social habits, but

Rüdiger Lainer and Gertraud Auer 1994

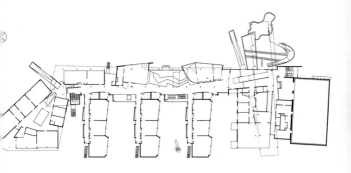

Favoriten to Inzersdorf

Rüdiger Lainer and Gertraud Auer 1994

architecture can aid or even avoid certain social processes.

IHA: Are you a Utopian?

Lainer: Yes, probably, despite what I know. It is a certain privilege you allow yourself. But in a heterogeneous reality, a global theory is not legitimate. There are a lot of nodes in the net and people choose one and make something out of it. There is no collective image of reality.

IHA: Does this conception of a heterogeneous reality have direct formal consequences for you?

Lainer: Architecture is a way to understand the world, and it entails a choice of form: the question is when do you choose that form? It is often done at the beginning; I try to do it at the end. I start with a story, with the complexity, with making the net. The choice of form comes out of understanding the relations, the morphological ideas – form is a result of intuition, of pragmatic fact, of morphological fact: of understanding the task in different ways, through images, through metaphors, all that can be related in a given situation – that becomes form, like Indians dancing around a totem. The final form-making process is then quite concentrated, quick and energetic.

ADDRESS 10., Absberggasse [45 S 13]
CLIENT Stadt Wien
COLOUR CONCEPT Oscar Putz
SIZE 18 classes, 5100 square metres net
COST ÖS 140 million
GETTING THERE U1 to Reumannplatz, then tram 67 to Schleiergasse
ACCESS by appointment

Rüdiger Lainer and Gertraud Auer 1994

Favoriten to Inzersdorf

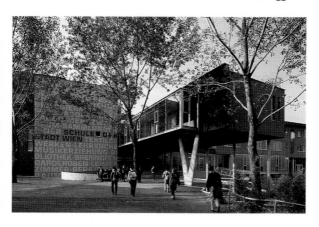

Rüdiger Lainer and Gertraud Auer 1994

Business Park Vienna

Office building is problematic in a city. Offices house the stage between manufacture and consumer and as such have little to offer the surrounding city apart from the odd bit of parkland and the reassuring symbols of financial growth. But business premises are invariably advertised as being 'close to the city centre', 'well connected to existing infrastructure': in other words, an urban image is essential.

This is also the case in the sparkling new Business Park Vienna. The offices are well planned, flexible, fully serviced, arranged in individually identifiable parts around three interior courtyards. The three u-shaped blocks along the Wienerbergallee are linked to the city by a glazed shopping mall which opens through to a green pedestrian route leading to the new hotel and golf course. Through the glazed court of the mall you can look up to the 22 storeys of the stubby tower at the front, which stands on one of the highest points in the city and 'enriches the skyline coming from the south autobahn, an emblem for Vienna'.

But it takes more than patent glazing to make an emblem. All the parts of the complex facing the new square in front of the mall are desperately trying to live up to their role of 'public face'. However, despite all the glass there is no transparency, which is not only due to the reflective coating – this building accepts no form but its own, the urban surroundings are at most a pleasant view from within.

ADDRESS 10., Wienerbergstrasse [43 S 10]
CLIENT Wienerberger Immobilien AG
ASSOCIATED ARCHITECTS Klaus Peter Erblich, Zachari Vesselinov, Manfred Hirschler, Peter Scheufler, Gerhard Schweighofer
GETTING THERE tram 65 to Windtenstrasse
ACCESS shops open, offices by appointment

Favoriten to Inzersdorf

Atelier 4 1990–1994

Wohnhausanlage Wienerberg Phase 2

The city planners of Vienna are on a mission. Their expressed aim of building 10,000 units of housing per year is exceptional by any standards. The underlying concern is demographic: after decades of population decline Vienna is growing, and social expectations are high – most people expect to have the option of a subsidised flat and the government is doing what it can to keep waiting lists as short as possible.

The new housing at the Wienerberg takes a cross-section of the last 15 years of architectural development in Vienna. The buildings of Phase 1, east of Otto-Probst-Strasse, were commissioned in 1982 and are largely undistinguished by any architectural effort with the possible exceptions of the section by Manfred Nehrer and a little yellow townhouse by Erich Bramhas. In the part across the road, the centre around Tesarekplatz and the housing projects on Otto-Probst-Strasse 22–34, Hugo-Meisl-Weg, Jungbauerweg, Sedlacek-Weg and August-Sigl-Strasse, it is very clear that the emphasis has shifted. The buildings are both individually more defined and function better as a considered whole.

The last phase of the development, to the south of Otto-Probst-Strasse, is still under construction but already shows some of the predictable elements of design like simple bold forms and strong colours which for better or worse have been established by example during the last seven or eight years.

The buildings of Phase 2 vary widely in their exterior design. There are the white Landvillen by Gustav Peichl dancing their geometrical dance along Hugo-Meisl-Weg. There are the red and blue blocks by Otto Steidle under tall trees at the back of Otto-Probst-Strasse 32–34, attached to the dense courtyard by Günther Oberhofer. Otto Steidle, who worked with Adolf Krischanitz and Herzog & De Meuron on the much-discussed Pilotengasse project, has also designed Otto-Probst-Strasse 28–30. Otto

Various architects 1990–1994, masterplan Otto Häuselmayer 1982

PUTZEREI

SONNEN-STUDIO

Various architects 1990–1994, masterplan Otto Häuselmayer 1982

Häuselmayer continues the white simplicity of the church on Tesarekplatz in his projects on Otto-Probst-Strasse 22–24 and at the back end of Otto-Probst-Strasse 26, butting up to the rather clumsy red and blue blocks by Werner Oberman. The corner of Otto-Probst-Platz, next to the pink building by Rudolf Lamprecht, is framed by the concave façade of the project by Helmut Wimmer.

The internal layout of subsidised flats is governed by so many regulations that it is difficult to achieve much variation. As a rule a flat is a flat – there must be defined rooms, and every square metre must have a designated function in order to receive subsidies. Some of the projects were originally planned with more undefined spaces, but had to change when the development was handed to a different housing association for execution. Another obstacle to change is the fact that the architect has no control of the flow of money; a saving in one area is more likely to go straight in to the developer's pocket than into supporting other solutions in another area.

The layout of the blocks is dense. The common theme is the internal courtyard or Hof, intended to bring an urban density to the greenfield development. However, as the area is pedestrianised and has no streets in an urban sense apart from the main throughway, the result is a curious mixture of urban proximity and the aspirations of a garden city: the individual four- to five-storey blocks are in part very close to each other, but at the same time no particular emphasis is placed on the areas between them which is simply covered by a flat lawn and a network of footpaths. The plan is shaped by two conflicting aims: the privacy of the suburban villa as an ideal living situation and the density of the city as a justification for a profitable development, in this case compounded by the visible difference of aesthetic approach between the various architects. The

Various architects 1990–1994, masterplan Otto Häuselmayer 1982

Various architects 1990–1994, masterplan Otto Häuselmayer 1982

tension between the two aims is obvious, but perhaps precisely this instability makes for an architectural and social environment which is not completely resolved and therefore open for development and change.

ADDRESS 10, Otto-Probst-Platz, Otto-Probst-Strasse, Hugo-Meisl-Weg, Tesarikplatz [44 T 11]
ARCHITECTS Otto Häuselmayer, Rudolf Lamprecht, Günther Oberhofer, Werner Oberman, Gustav Peichl, Otto Steidle, Helmut Wimmer
CLIENTS Wien Süd, GP, GESIBA, GSG
GETTING THERE U1 to Reumannplatz, then tram 67 to Otto-Probst-Platz
ACCESS to grounds

Various architects 1990–1994, masterplan Otto Häuselmayer 1982

Various architects 1990–1994, masterplan Otto Häuselmayer 1982

Church Tesarekplatz

The Wienerberg area has been one of the most important concentrations of housing development over the last ten years. Otto Häuselmayer won the masterplanning competition in 1980, and in 1994 they are still building – eventually there will be 2100 new flats. The area is well provided for. The new local centre is formed by the communal buildings around the Tesarekplatz, a school, nursery school and church as well as a café and shopping centre.

Häuselmayer's church is modest in scale and materials, as well as in its symbolic aspirations. It faces the square with a glazed entrance which opens directly on to the pavement, no level change, no space of transition. It is rendered white inside and out, and capped by a timber and sheet metal vault carried by a thin steel lattice held up by internal columns, leaving a glazed clerestory strip around the main church room. This lifting of the roof by a strip of natural light is a feature of many modern churches. In this case it remains mundane, the hint in a celestial direction is kept general as if to avoid the embarrassment of explicit declarations of faith. The church cannot be too specific for fear of becoming exclusive, so the main symbolic feature is the room for the congregation, the common room, little different from a regular community hall. The abundance of space is all that remains of symbolic potential – financial common sense dictates that no-one would go to the expense of leaving a three-storey building empty so there must be something there, architectural proof of the existence of God.

ADDRESS 10., Tesarekplatz 2 [44 T 11]
ENGINEERS Wolfdietrich Ziesel and Karl Schebesta
GETTING THERE U1 to Reumannplatz, then tram 67 to Tesarekplatz
ACCESS open during church services

Otto Häuselmayer 1992

Favoriten to Inzersdorf

Otto Häuselmayer 1992

School Tesarekplatz

Diagonally across from the church another expanse of white render shields the new town centre. Tesarekplatz is an austere little square, covered in uniform grey paving stones and enclosed on three sides by almost blank white walls. Glittering in the sun, Peichl's school lies there like an enigmatic but benign white elephant, grinning broadly with its strange roofline, lifted at the edges to give higher perimeter windows and better light to the classrooms.

The plan is organised around a rectangular internal court, encircled by a corridor with the classrooms around the outside. The gymnasium is in a square building at the back with a concave roof, linked to the main building by a courtyard and two small corridors.

Outside on the pavement, in front of the entrance is the *peichl* itself, the point, the cone or, in this case, pyramid which inevitably tops off most of Peichl's buildings.

ADDRESS 10., Tesarekplatz [44 T 11]
CLIENT Stadt Wien
SIZE 14 classes
GETTING THERE U1 to Reumannplatz, then tram 67 to Tesarekplatz or Otto-Probst-Platz
ACCESS during school hours

Gustav Peichl 1992

Gustav Peichl 1992

Kindertagesheim Tesarekplatz

Between the church and the school lies Tesar's nursery school. It is connected to the square by a little walled forecourt behind a concrete screen and an italianate steel gate. Again Tesarekplatz is faced with a blank white wall, it is unclear whether this is by public agreement or by conspiracy.

Inside a tiled corridor goes off to the right of the double- height entry hall, a marble tiled stair goes up to the first floor gallery. The playrooms along the corridor open towards the back, to the playground and the garden. The materials are economical, white rendered walls, white painted steel. The walled courtyard to the front is surrounded by the offices of the administration, the walled garden to the back catches the children as soon as they run out – this is not a place which tries to modify its institutional nature. Full control is maintained at all times, reassuring to the parents if not necessarily to the children.

ADDRESS 10., Tesarekplatz 3 [44 T 11]
CLIENT Stadt Wien
SIZE seven classes
GETTING THERE U1 to Reumannplatz, then tram 67 to Tesarekplatz
ACCESS none

Favoriten to Inzersdorf

Heinz Tesar 1992

Favoriten to Inzersdorf

Heinz Tesar 1992

Siedlung Traviatagasse

Life does not have to be sweet. There is depression, there is depravity, there is death. But to build like this …

Next to the gargantuan geometry and blank surfaces of this housing scheme, everything ordinary looks out of place. The parts by Buck & Giencke and Lautner/Scheifinger/Szedenik/Schindler are fighting a loosing battle to ameliorate the thunderous presence of the parts by Abraham and Pruscha, whose insistent, heavy constructions verge on the paranoid.

Despite the fortified west wall preventing any enjoyment of the evening light, Lautner/Scheifinger/Szedenik/Schindler (Pfarrgasse 67–73) have made a valuable contribution to the semi-urban surroundings with their varied transitions from public to private. There are east-facing raised private gardens to the back of the four-storey block, and above the gardens a series of cut-outs, painted fleshy pink, step back into the white façade to give all flats a useable external area. The second row of three-storey terraced houses have clear divisions between each of the repeated units and again a variety of connections between internal and external spaces.

Buck & Giencke's long block (Traviatagasse 21–29) closes off the area to the north, opening to the south in a cascade of balconies and terraces down to a long square. However, despite its strict and somewhat formalist symmetry, it looks positively whimsical next to the neighbouring sinister monoliths.

The units of the three white terraces by Abraham, at the eastern border of the scheme, are divided by head-high garden walls, solid concrete 30 cm thick. It is as if the architect wants to be *inside* the material itself, existential doubt kept at bay by sheer solidity. The entrance doors are arbitrary openings squeezed between the crushing forms of the staircase

Masterplan by Raimund Abraham 1991

cylinder and the overhanging square bay. In both the parts by Pruscha and by Abraham living takes place vertically, the rooms are stacked with few possibilities of connection and a lot of space taken up by vertical circulation.

Carl Pruscha's windowless fortress of red concrete block (Kolpingstrasse 1–7) is traversed by the axes of two pedestrian streets, lined down the middle with creaking poplars. In the deep internal courtyards all sound is coolly minimised, galvanised platforms on in-situ concrete columns hover overhead, severing the connection between life in the flats and the ground. It is simple, consistent and elegantly put together, but leaden, with no resonance to the minimalism, not even acoustically. The associations are too far away, nothing of the surroundings is gathered in by the building. On the contrary, everything familiar is kept out by the geometry and the overwhelming mass.

Walter Chramosta (architect and critic): If De Chirico had seen this he would have painted differently.

ADDRESS 23., Traviatagasse, Pfarrgasse, Kolpingstrasse [55 V 10]
ARCHITECTS Raimund Abraham, Walter Buck/Uta Giencke, Günther Lautner/Peter Scheifinger/Rudolf Szedenik/Cornelia Schindler, Carl Pruscha
CLIENT GSG
SIZE Abraham 39 + 20 units; Buck/Giencke 36 units; Lautner/Scheifinger/Szedenik 36 units; Pruscha 36 units
GETTING THERE Badner Bahn from Oper to Gutheil-Schoder-Gasse, then bus 16A to Traviatagasse
ACCESS to grounds

Masterplan by Raimund Abraham 1991

Meidling to Mödling

Gartenhotel Altmansdorf

This new hotel is the last chapter in the long and varied history of its site. An Augustinian monastery in the 14th century, it was converted into the palace of the Frankl family in 1819, added to in 1976 to make room for the Dr Karl Renner Institute, and run as a hotel from 1981. Across the road is Siedlung Hoffingergasse by Josef Frank and Erich Faber from 1924. Most of this history is still visible. The 1976 building has been renovated and included in the new hotel, the overgrown gothic 19th-century garden can be seen through the full-height glazing of the new restaurant.

The sales manager who showed me around kept repeating the word 'transparency' as if it were a magic formula, which in this case might well be true. The new building adds to the whole ensemble while remaining open to the older parts, and the 'transparency' is consistent throughout and instrumental in tying it all together.

On entry you see right through the reception hall, across the lower-level hotel restaurant, out into the old garden beyond. The kitchen is shared by the hotel and the *à la carte* restaurant in the restored Orangerie, it faces the forecourt of the hotel, making the inner workings of the place immediately visible. The connection between the old and the new building are by open bridges across public lounges. Nothing is hidden.

Compare this with the ANA Hotel in the new Palais Corso on the Ringstrasse – hotel-chain design with a no doubt huge expense gone in to the interior mock Rococo fittings, resulting in no more than a caricature of elegance. Hotel Altmansdorf takes a very different approach. All fittings in the rooms are built in, simple, imaginative and very well made. The absence of standard hotel-room furniture is refreshing, everything is special, making maximum use of the limited space available.

The interior focuses as much as possible on the attractions of the outside. The rooms on the garden side have a little loggia, an openable

Michael Schluder and Hanns Kastner 1994

Meidling to Mödling

Michael Schluder and Hanns Kastner 1994

seating area facing the garden, and the rooms on the street side have full-height glazing looking out over Frank's housing. The bathrooms are open, glazed to the rest of the room, you can even have a view of the garden while you shower. These fantastic details and the connection to the surroundings is also a point of economy for the hotel: it gives a sense of something extraordinary, of being somewhere else, away from home, without having to resort to expensive finishes and reproduction furniture.

ADDRESS 12., Hoffingergasse 26–28 [43 S 9]
CLIENT SPÖ Österreich
STRUCTURAL ENGINEER Oskar Graf
COLOUR CONCEPT Oskar Putz
SIZE new building: 57 rooms, 410 square metres seminar rooms, 220-seat restaurant, 25 parking spaces
GETTING THERE tram 62 to Altmannsdorfer Strasse/Hetzendorf
ACCESS open

Michael Schluder and Hanns Kastner 1994

Michael Schluder and Hanns Kastner 1994

School Rohrwassergasse

This school is set in old parkland behind Hetzendorf Palace, new and white among the trees. It consists of two blocks: one rectangular block along Rohrwassergasse containing teaching rooms for special subjects with the gymnasium at the end, and one a long curved block with two levels of classrooms and offices. The classrooms all face the old park, and from the double-height 'living room' of the school, the hall between the two blocks, there is a wide view through to the trees and grass of the outside playground. The entrance to the hall follows the curved wing and brings you in along the side, leaving the hall and whoever is in it undisturbed, unlike, for example, Czech's school (see page 136) where you come directly in to occupy the centre. The gallery above protrudes out above the entrance with a view out to a row of concrete numerals rising out of the ground in a precarious and rather patronising countdown to entering the school: the number 5 is still lying on its back and the number 1 finally stands erect as one of the columns of the entrance canopy.

Like their school in Pernerstorferstrasse, the strength of this building by Nehrer + Medek is not in its rather schematic detailing but in its clear and considered connection to the surrounding site.

ADDRESS 12., Rohrwassergasse 2/Margarete-Seeman-Weg 1 [42 s 8]
CLIENT Stadt Wien
STRUCTURAL ENGINEER Günther Urban
SIZE 13 classes, Volksschule
GETTING THERE tram 62 to Schloß Hetzendorf
ACCESS by arrangement

Manfred Nehrer and Reinhard Medek 1993

Manfred Nehrer and Reinhard Medek 1993

Brunner Strasse

It should not be possible. All the people who complain about the restrictions of the subsidised housing industry will tell you it is not possible, to stretch reality this far.

IHA: With the amount of building currently going on, are you optimistic about the future of architecture in Vienna?

Helmut Richter: Optimism and pessimism ... No. I don't think in those terms.

Brunner Strasse is a heavily trafficked road connecting the south-western suburbs to the autobahn. The main element of Richter's scheme is a full-height glass screen which protects the houses from the traffic noise, behind which a series of walkways gives access to the flats. These fairfaced concrete galleries are open to the air, covered by a translucent fibreglass roof only punctured by the bright red steel-clad lift shaft and the tops of the staircases, wrapped in bright red rubberised sheet. Along the road the glass is constantly shifting, bending slightly, and the size and organisation of the buildings behind also change, from solid façade to red lift to full opening into the gardens and back to solid. There is no schematic repetition; every change of situation in the internal organisation and in the context is dealt with as an individual challenge within the whole. And all along you can see the thinking which made it possible, the constant attention given to every new problem. The glass wall gives privacy from the passing cars, the changing angles ensures the reflection which makes the glass opaque. It is only when you are head-on or close-up that you can see through into the semi-private zone behind. Because the galleries are open to the air, the detailing of the glass can be minimal, held only by a slender framework of round galvanised steel sections.

Helmut Richter 1990

Meidling to Mödling

Helmut Richter 1990

The apartment plans have been twisted off the predictable orthogonal grid, forming a sequence from front to back around a storage-cube in the middle of the hallway and an internal lightwell. A fine tension is induced by the angled walls, which allow the spaces to affect each other while retaining the definition of the individual rooms.

The materials span from in-situ concrete and toughened glass to rubber and painted fibre panels, with galvanised mesh and perspex screens to the loggias and aluminium-framed sliding doors to the living rooms. The man-made materials succeed in drawing on the local associations of this industrial city periphery, turning accidental and unimportant memories into something familiar which gives new meaning to both the domestic interior and its immediate surroundings.

Meidling to Mödling

ADDRESS 23., Brunner Strasse 26–32, Autofabrikgasse 7 [54 V 7]
ENGINEER Wolfgang Vasko
CLIENT ÖS
SIZE 61 units, 61–106 square metres
COST ÖS 60 million
GETTING THERE train S1, S2 or R10 to Atzgersdorf-Mauer, then bus 60A or 66A to Brunner Strasse
ACCESS none

Helmut Richter 1990

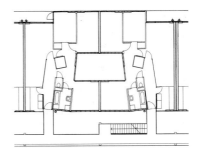

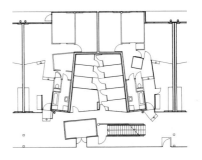

Meidling to Mödling

Helmut Richter 1990

Breitenfurter Strasse

There is a certain brand of insistent post-modernism which always makes me think of the comic *Asterix – city planner*, not just because of the images of the rendered Roman buildings with their pitched-roof formality, but also because of its grandiose intentions.

Officius: Please tell us, oh Caesar, what that is supposed to be?
Caesar: These Gauls think they can resist the Roman civilisation just because they have a magic potion which gives them superhuman strength, and because they are protected and fed by a forest. But I will force them to accept this civilisation! The forest will fall, and in its place will be a park! And finally a Roman settlement will besiege the village, and it will be nothing but an insignificant suburb, which will adapt or disappear!
(Goscinny and Uderzo, *Asterix xvii – Die Trabantenstadt* [Delta Verlag, Stuttgart 1993], pages 4–5)

Nothing short of faith is required to believe that an environment of classical forms and references has a civilising effect on a barbaric mankind. Nonetheless, as Roman settlements go, the one on Breitenfurter Strasse in the 23rd district of Vienna is a splendid achievement. The parts by Krier, the triangular block by the aqueduct, the circular central piazza and the most recent block at the end, are undisputedly the high points, with the parts by Gebhardt along the road and by Wachberger along the brook to the south little more than a coloured background vaguely in tune with the efforts of the Master.

Krier's pieces have an air of lament, materialised in the large sculpture of two pained and stunted torsos in the central court. And edifice after edifice, cornice upon pediment upon colonnade rises against the sky in

Rob Krier with Hedwig Wachberger and Peter Gebhart 1988

Rob Krier with Hedwig Wachberger and Peter Gebhart 1988

defiance of the unbearable banality of life. The themes set out by Krier are then followed by the others in more diagrammatical solutions. But please explain, oh Caesar. Stair 19 serves six units and stair 20 serves eight. Stair 19 is huge, centrally placed, with a portico and sweeping stairs going up, stair 20 is tucked in under the building through a plain little hall. The elements of the complex are subjected to a differentiation which is unrelated to their functional meaning, and it makes me wonder …

Two boys were walking the colonnade around the round piazza, the middle of which is occupied by a tree. They trace lines already drawn through centuries of theories of organisation – axis, centre, periphery. This is also a moral question: what understanding of reality develops from walking this circle?

Obelix: You are scaring the boars! They are not used to strangers.
Quadratus [Caesar's architect]: Kindly let me work in peace!

(Goscinny and Uderzo, *op.cit.*, page 8)

ADDRESS 23., Breitenfurter Strasse 380–413 [53 V 6]
CLIENT Gemeinde Wien
STRUCTURAL ENGINEER Roland Martinz
SIZE 300 units, 120 by Krier
GETTING THERE train S1, S2 or R10 to Liesing
ACCESS to grounds and shops

Rob Krier with Hedwig Wachberger and Peter Gebhart 1988

Rob Krier with Hedwig Wachberger and Peter Gebhart 1988

Brunnergasse

Hermann Czech has built a small settlement in Perchtoldsdorf, one of the towns just to the south of Vienna. It is an assembly of seven T-shaped plans and two larger buildings on a slope to the north-west of Brunnergasse, planned with user participation. It strikes a fine balance between the structure given by repeating the same element, and the variation provided by the topography of the slope and the irregular layout of the houses, which also gives the interiors different orientations. The same balance controls the expression of the difference between the individual buildings.

The loadbearing external walls gave the possibility of an open internal structure, consisting only of a couple of columns in the middle of each flat. Tenants could decide on the internal layout and the size and position of windows, limited by the maximum structural opening which remains as a depression in the external render, the only embellishment on the simple pink façade. All flats have access to the garden, directly or via a brown timber stair. The recessed window fields and the repeated units leaves the impression of a system, but a system altered in such a way as to give room for differentiation. Czech does not fall for the temptation of making these differences obvious by a multitude of colours and forms: the suppleness is contained within the overall idea; his is an architecture of suggestion.

ADDRESS Brunnergasse, 2380 Perchtoldsdorf [64 Y 6]
CLIENT 'Alpenland' for Stadtgemeinde Perchtoldsdorf
SIZE 57 units, 60–100 square metres
GETTING THERE S1 or S2 to Perchtoldsdorf Haltestelle, then bus 257 to Brunnergasse
ACCESS to grounds

Hermann Czech 1994

Hermann Czech 1994

Mödlinger Bühne

Mödling is a beautiful town outside Vienna, worth going to see just for its historic centre on the wooded slopes of the Föhrenberge. Elsa Prochazka's cinema foyer in the renovated town theatre is an added bonus.

Behind the historical façade, finely assembled sheets of polished oak clad the new inside of the old building. All new corners are mitred. The floor is a pale, grey-black striped terrazzo, with an orange leather bench at one end, and mirrors bolted to the wall at the other end where the old stairs go up to the first circle. Straight ahead is a wall of opaque enamelled glass, behind which is the cloakroom, hidden for cinema and opened for theatre performances, one of the servicing elements which are specialised for the dual function of cinema and theatre. The foyer is lit by clear naked bulbs strewn across the white ceiling, embarrassingly bright but giving an atmosphere of expectation, of dressing rooms, of stage lights, in a confident balance between grandiosity and precision.

Meidling to Mödling

ADDRESS Babenbergerstrasse 5, 2340 Mödling [65 ZB 7]
CLIENT Stadtgemeinde Mödling
GETTING THERE S1 or S2 to Mödling
ACCESS open

Renovation Elsa Prochazka 1994

Renovation Elsa Prochazka 1994

Hietzing and Penzing

Nobilegasse

This well-mannered housing block in the 15th district is distinguished by its subtle and intelligent relationship with the existing buildings. The problem of fitting five floors into the height of the four on either side is solved with the help of the natural slope of the street, the increased density of the new block is camouflaged by the necessary stepping of the row of buildings down the slope and by making the new windows the same size and proportion as the existing. Where the blue liftshaft and staircase splits the yellow building there is a half-storey step within the building itself.

The flat layouts stay within the limitations of subsidised housing, various configurations of rectangular rooms separated by their designated functions. The façade is kept neutral, divided into the classical rusticated base, middle and top, with a perforated overhang at the parapet which decorates the building front with long stripes of light when the sun is at the right angle.

ADDRESS 15., Nobilegasse 51–53 [31 O/P 9]
CLIENT 'Familienhilfe'
GETTING THERE tram 49 to Johnstrasse
ACCESS none

Friedrich Kurrent 1987

Friedrich Kurrent 1987

Muthsamgasse

This building wants to be taken seriously as a town-house. The tall, rendered base, the inclined walls flanking the ceremonial entrance stair, the ten five-storey hollow half-columns running up the front, all give the exterior an air of self-conscious grandiosity. Seen from down the street, in perspective, the fibre-reinforced pilasters make a smooth black wall, with a texture like soapstone.

The inside, however, is different. There are two types of flat, a result of the discrepancy of conviction between the architect and the client. Anton Schweighofer has an ongoing preoccupation with an ideal plan, the idea of which is to retain a degree of choice in how the interior is used. The client, a housing association, was concerned with rentability and wanted to stick to the conventional plan of designated rooms. As a result, the corner flat has the conventional large living room with kitchen/dining room off it and three smaller bedrooms, and the flats at each end are adaptations of Schweighofer's ideal plan. This is ideally square, with five equally spaced rooms, one in each corner and one in the middle. Between each of the corner rooms is a smaller ancillary room containing entrance, kitchen, bathroom and the last opening out on to the balcony. This principle is most consistently realised in Schweighofer's housing scheme in Gatterburggasse.

ADDRESS 14., Muthsamgasse 3 [30 0 8]
CLIENT GWV
SIZE 27 units
GETTING THERE tram 49 to Reinlgasse, then tram 10 to Laurentiusplatz
ACCESS none

Anton Schweighofer 1986

Anton Schweighofer 1986

Waidhausenstrasse

This housing scheme is perfect. It is a regular six-storey block, typical of the area, divided into a front and a back block by an internal courtyard and a small communal building. The construction is the usual concrete frame and rendered external walls, in this case painted deep pink and orange with a pale green set-back top storey. The finishes are modest, render and paint inside, standard timber window frames, terrazzo tiles and a little bit of steel. It has all the discipline of an inner-city building, conforming to roof lines, building lines and prescribed density.

However, perfection in this case is not matching an outside ideal, but is built into the house itself. With variation that never seems contrived, the exterior responds to the interior: breaking the flat surface of the façade, twisting it slightly this way and that to catch or avoid a view, opening it for a loggia and closing it again with wired glass for privacy. Everything is finely detailed: slender galvanised steel and different textures of glass, the shallow rounded steps in the entrance hall – more like crossing natural terrain than walking up a stair. No device is taken for granted, everything is considered, chosen and constructed with the same sensitivity. What lacks an obvious function is restrained and neutral, making a whole where all individual decisions seem logical, but brought together without a preconceived external form. Instead of the schematic clarity of a modernist grid or the limitations of a postmodernist classical reference, there is a unique and confident complexity.

ADDRESS 14., Waidhausenstrasse 24 [29 O/P 6]
CLIENT WE
COST ÖS 28 million
GETTING THERE tram 49 to Waidhausenstrasse
ACCESS none

Rüdiger Lainer and Gertraud Auer 1991

Rüdiger Lainer and Gertraud Auer 1991

School Kinkplatz

Helmut Richter's building for a school in the 14th district puts a lot of contemporary Viennese architecture into perspective. There is no real tradition of dry steel construction in Vienna, no tradition of prefabrication. Most of what is being built, certainly most of the public housing, conforms for practical reasons to the expectations of the clients, the housing associations, and construction is limited to rendered blockwork and the odd steel detail. Against this background, Richter's achievement appears even more impressive. It is an individual *tour-de-force*, no doubt destined to be the object of much criticism and professional envy.

IHA: Are you satisfied?
Helmut Richter: Satisfied? Why should I not be satisfied … ?

Built on a steeply sloping triangular site next to a churchyard, the plan is more-or-less a straightforward diagram. Three long blocks face the existing buildings to the north, connected by a perpendicular corridor or gallery at the south end. The three levels of the gallery all look out to the hills south of the city, through the enormous sloping sheets of glass which cover the triple gymnasium and the indoor vestibule. The glass roofs and the steel construction carrying them, with a free span of over 25 metres, are the most striking elements of the building. Apparently the spending on the glass roof was possible because of the savings made by the engineer on the concrete construction: by removing half the amount of concrete and replacing it with a more carefully considered system of steel bracing, money could be released into other areas. In the context of how the construction process normally works in Vienna, there are two remarkable aspects to this, firstly that the engineer was involved to such a large degree, and secondly that the architect had enough influence on the client to deter-

Hietzing and Penzing

Helmut Richter 1994

mine where the savings went – normally they would go back to the client as profit. In the end, according to Richter, this school did not cost any more per square metre than Lainer's (see page 152), which for all its innovations generally uses more standard methods of construction.

Two structural principles are used in the two glass halls: the frame above the gymnasium is basically an A-frame; the one over the vestibule, where the site narrows and there is no room for such wide ground supports, is cantilevered from the edge of the floor slab with ties down to the foundations below. Different situation, different construction.

The three classroom blocks are made with in-situ columns and beams and precast floor elements, clad with corrugated sheet steel and stabilised by external and internal cross-bracing. There is a glazed fire escape stair at the end of each block. The structure is left bare internally and all services are visible: each classroom has its service riser; horizontal distribution is through the corridors, keeping the teaching spaces as clear as possible. Corridor walls are yellow, overhead cable trays blue. The lift shaft is bright red, painted concrete on the inside and rubberised sheet on the outside. The rest of the building is all natural colours, the greys and silvers of concrete, steel and aluminium, and the green shimmer of double glass.

Wolf Prix: Architects believe that architecture is discussed and that everyone is focused on architects – they are really very naive to think this way. People play with architects right now. And they play with architecture.

IHA: But architects take it.

Prix: Yes. And I think the most remarkable attitude that we have now is obedience. There is no spirit to invent things, there is no spirit to create new boundaries, or to push the edge, there's no attitude to be honest,

Helmut Richter 1994

to be tough, in the sense of standing by the project. I don't blame them, because if you're doing projects like this [points to a model of a recent Coop Himmelblau project], and you are responsible for a lot of people and so on … But this is a culture which expresses the attitude of the whole society.

The school in Waidhausenstrasse is an exception. Despite the obvious fascination with the construction and Richter's professed admiration for British hi-tech, this building has very little of the technological coquetry of, say, Michael Hopkins, where the one-off details in the end are more-or-less hand-crafted – the methods and materials used in the school are simple and repeatable. It gets its power from a visible consistency, each decision is a consequence of the last and no compromises are made along the way. Changes yes, compromises no. Every element and its relation to the next remains clearly defined throughout the self-appointed marathon challenge. Self-appointed because it was not the client who asked Richter for a 40-metre south-facing span of glass, or steel cladding and external cross-bracing. This is a municipal school, not headquarters for a prestigious insurance company. However, it is also the only building I have come across in Vienna which is so strongly and obviously a personal gesture of defiance.

ADDRESS 14., Kinkplatz 21 [29 0 6]
CLIENT Stadt Wien
ENGINEER Wolfgang Vasko
SIZE Doppelhauptschule, 12 + 8 classes for approximately 800 students
GETTING THERE tram 49 to Waidhausenstrasse
ACCESS by appointment

Hietzing and Penzing

Helmut Richter 1994

Helmut Richter 1994

School Hietzinger Hauptstrasse

An existing school and Kindergarten in Ober-St-Veit has been extended by a yellow glass cube. The extension, which contains three new class-rooms, offices, library and a lift-tower, clad on two sides with enamelled glass sheets, has been the subject of much local controversy. Such is the way here: anything new and sharp is criticised with great vigour, until the criticisms themselves have made the building so familiar that its removal would be received with as many protests as its erection. It happened with the Kunsthalle and it will no doubt happen here. And quite rightly so. Prochazka's new building, though in itself disciplined, revital-ises the old school and its stuffy surroundings.

The most obviously vigorous element is the yellow glass on the outside. Vigorous but not insensitive, even this seemingly foreign element absorbs and expresses its context in the uneven divisions of the glass panels which divide the building into the classical base, middle and top, and in the size and proportion of the windows which continue the fenestration of the old building in the same pale green colour. The precisely assembled inte-riors, plywood and laminate, beautiful but nonetheless industrial mate-rials, glass, unmediated by beads and skirtings, the sharp delineation of surfaces and the determined precision with which they come together, all result in a provoking clarity which would disappoint any vague senti-mental expectations of a confirmation of the past.

ADDRESS 13., Hietzinger Hauptstrasse 166–168 [41 Q 6]
ENGINEER Ewald Pachler
SIZE 6 classes (extension)
GETTING THERE U4 to Ober St Veit or tram 58 from Westbahnhof to Verbindungsbahn, then bus 53B to Wolfrathplatz
ACCESS by appointment

Hietzing and Penzing

Elsa Prochazka 1994

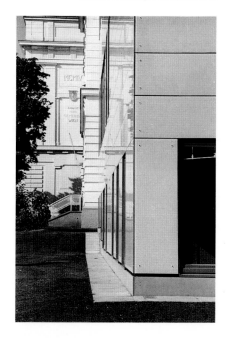

Hietzing and Penzing

Elsa Prochazka 1994

Käthe Leichter-Hof

Viennese architects have great difficulty forgetting the Karl-Marx-Hof. This famous 'super-block' by Karl Ehn from 1930 which has just been restored to its former yellow-and-red glory, a kilometre long with 1382 flats, keeps getting wheeled out as a reference to justify various kinds of projects, from decorative homage to blatant over-development.

Käthe-Leichter-Hof is a bit of both. It is a relatively large and relatively dense housing project, 174 flats, eight storeys towards Hietzinger Kai and a more modest five towards the quiet Auhofstrasse, looking deceptively small from the outside. Karl-Marx-Hof is clearly visible in the interior of the block, vertical balcony-stacks drawn in blue against pink render, trying to break down and mediate the large scale. It has the familiar postmodern symptoms like cut-out steel sheet pediments above the lift doors and stripes of a fleshy stone cladding to the base, but the scale and density of the layout as a whole is interesting. Rather than an open court inside, this is more varied, more compact, which results in a number of different in-between spaces. The surrounding tall buildings all have different terraces and balconies, not really well ordered, more a benign, recognisable expediency. There are different ways through, round balconies pivoting the corners, everywhere a different solution or arrangement has been differently dealt with, but the result is a surprising variation rather than confusion.

ADDRESS 13., Auhofstrasse 152–156/Hietzinger Kai 201–205 [29 P 6]
CLIENT WP
SIZE 174 units, 144 parking spaces
COST ÖS 10,673 per square metre
GETTING THERE U4 to Ober-St-Veit
ACCESS to grounds

T Melicher, G Schwalm-Theiss, H Gressenbauer with W Fürtner 1988

T Melicher, G Schwalm-Theiss, H Gressenbauer with W Fürtner 1988

Ottakring to Neuwaldegg

Austria Tabak

One-third laboratories for Austria Tabak and two-thirds rental offices, this modest-scale inner city office building is planned around a flexible grid within which walls can be moved to suit any tenant's requirements. Flexibility is the main priority of the construction: services run in floor and ceiling and are accessible throughout, heating and electricity are installed under the windows to provide outlets in every office regardless of the partitions.

The front and back use different structural systems: as half of the ground-floor columns had to come out to allow for a loading bay, the structure on the back is effectively hung from a truss at roof level to make spans twice as long.

The precision of the exterior aluminium cladding and self-supporting glass is a welcome break from the ubiquitous rendered façades of subsidised housing. The plan is simple. The long block is broken up by three internal lightwells which, together with continuous strip windows and open-ended corridors, ensure that you are never far from light. The offices all face out and are arranged along two internal corridors. There is a staircase adjacent to each lightwell, two circular and one square. The geometry seems schematic but, as in the new schools by Nehrer + Medek, the schematic geometrical decision has been consciously followed through into the details and appears well-ordered, generous and consistent.

ADDRESS 16., Hasnerstrasse 127/Koppstrasse 116 [30 N 8]
CLIENT Austria Tabak
SIZE 14,500 square metres, 71 parking spaces
COST ÖS 288 million
GETTING THERE tram 46 to Ottakring
ACCESS by appointment

Manfred Nehrer and Reinhard Medek 1994

Manfred Nehrer and Reinhard Medek 1994

Frauenfelderstrasse

This block of flats and maisonettes was built for the private rental market rather than as subsidised housing. The financing meant there was more time and money, allowing a different approach to the design. Henke and Schreieck are both former students of Roland Rainer, an influence visible in the rigour of design and unsentimental use of materials, as well as an interest in reducing things to a minimum. But despite the strict discipline and minimalism of the building there is no repetition, no abstract rule. Every situation is handled in a different way.

IHA: When I saw this building I thought: here is a simplicity of material which gives associations to things outside of what is constructed. Not through direct visual reference, but at the edge of the glass, where the material comes to an end, a thought continues. Is that an intention from your side?

Dieter Henke: Yes. For instance the big façade is such a strong element in itself, it pushes everything else away. So the question was how to somehow keep it under control, and we decided to fix one half of the sliding shutters. But the apartment is only 4.5 metres wide, what is it like to be there when the one half is closed? It was a long and difficult decision, we made models to simulate it, the distances between the louvre blades, and finally we decided that it was no problem: it gives privacy to the flat and it keeps the façade more under control, without it becoming too busy. But the decision was always from the inside. Most of the work on this project, right from the start of the competition, was really like this: from the inside out. For us that is very important; the building springs from the inside living quality of the apartments.

Marta Schreieck: We wanted the relatively small flats to appear as large

Dieter Henke and Marta Schreieck 1993

Dieter Henke and Marta Schreieck 1993

as possible, so there are no fully enclosed spaces, but dissolved surfaces, ceiling, wall and floor. It is important that you can trace how the house is constructed, the materials are just placed next to each other, everything is readable.

IHA: Would it be possible to make something like that within the frame of social housing?

Schreieck: Not the interiors. You could make the elementary room and leave everything else out, and maybe the double sliding façade … The façade was an experiment, we developed it with the builders. Nothing like that existed and the louvre blades are specially made. That quality of execution is obviously not possible in social housing. But you could make it simpler.

IHA: Is minimalism a moral choice?

Henke: No. It's about naming different things and getting to know them.

Schreieck: Simplicity to me is not enough, something must be complex in order to be simplified. We always try to look at things from different sides when we are developing a concept, and only when several factors are discovered can you make a right decision. It is not just about achieving simplicity – we are of course disposed to try to reduce as much as possible, but I see nothing moral behind that. It is more a wish to bring something to a point where it really takes a position.

ADDRESS 17., Frauenfelderstrasse 14 [18 L 8]
CLIENT ÖBV
SIZE 40 units and shop and showrooms
OTHER Bauherrenpreis (awarded to the client) Preis der ZV 1993
GETTING THERE tram 43 to Hernals
ACCESS none

Dieter Henke and Marta Schreieck 1993

Dieter Henke and Marta Schreieck 1993

Promenadegasse 44

Neuwaldegg on the north-west edge of Vienna is a strange, incongruous area of villas, housing estates and vineyards. Promenadegasse 44 is a stocky little building, tucked away under a curved metal-sheet-clad roof. It is set on the edge of a hill and extends down from two storeys on the front to four at the back, containing seven large maisonettes. The common staircases cut through the entire house, theoretically letting you all the way through like one of the area's many open stairs connecting street to street.

The building's detailing is rather awkward, as if what should have been large is too small, and what should have been small is too large. The two-storey front to Promenadegasse relates to the scale of the villas, the four-storey back to the housing blocks, a result of the steep site and an imaginative contribution to an area where 19th-century cast-concrete tree trunks and neo-classical porticoes appear next to 1970s' prefabricated housing on the forested hills.

ADDRESS 17., Promenadegasse 44 [18 L 7]
CLIENT 'Schönere Zukunft'
STRUCTURAL ENGINEER Franz Toporek
SIZE seven units, total 710 square metres
GETTING THERE tram 43 to Neuwaldegg
ACCESS none

Eva Ceska and Friedrich Priesner 1992

Ottakring to Neuwaldegg

Eva Ceska and Friedrich Priesner 1992

Wittgensteingründe

The house occupying the so-called 'Wittgensteingründe' is clearly a spoken house. The architects' own account of the building (*Neuer Wiener Wohnbau* [Löcker Verlag, Wien 1992] page 148) is an account of their conversation: about the 'mutation of a hillside, the processes of autonomous objects, the possible possibility of habitation'.

The elements of the building itself are locked in a tense, discordant sequence along a steep hillside, framed by trees. The immateriality of the rendered surfaces makes the argument abstract, form following form, from red to yellow to polished black. Now other people have moved in, with their own mild protest of flower pots, lawn sprinklers and garden furniture.

ADDRESS 17, Neuwaldegger Strasse 38A [18 K 7]
CLIENT SEG
SIZE 17 units
GETTING THERE tram 43 to Neuwaldegg
ACCESS none

Max Rieder, Wolfgang Tschapeller, Hans Peter Wörndl 1990

Ottakring to Neuwaldegg

Max Rieder, Wolfgang Tschapeller, Hans Peter Wörndl 1990

Alsergrund, Währing, Döbling

School Köhlergasse

Hollein's school is located on a very steep hill. It has two internal court-yards, the upper one covered with earth, the lower one larger and covered with brick pavers. The building ends in a sheer wall towards Gentzgasse, a four-storey drop from a roof garden. It makes an interesting comparison to the Haas-Haus on Stock-im-Eisen-Platz, not least because these are the only large buildings Hollein has completed in Vienna.

From the entrance the view spreads everywhere: up, down, through, towards light, into courtyards, corridors, temples, turrets, across an inte-rior landscape of construction. It is immediately explorable in a very different way to the Haas-Haus, which presents itself as understandable on first glance but then gets lost in complications. Here the elements are left to themselves, in all their glorious variations of mimicry, and only after a while do they come together in a many-faceted whole which plays perfectly alongside the children. It is also worn, which gives it an air of credibility. The school seems to play a fairer game than the more glam-orous building in the city centre, but even here Hollein provides no handles for grasping the whole, no symmetry, no unmistakable hierarchy. Or rather, he provides too many. Why that red steel sheet by the entrance? Why the tempietta with the starry dome and the rusticated base? Why the four floors of a fortress towering above the street? What you are up against here, rather than the comfort of a predictable solution, is the terri-fying threat of having to choose for yourself, or maybe in this case rather to learn, how to understand the environment you are in.

ADDRESS 18., Köhlergasse 9 [19 L 10]
CLIENT Stadt Wien
GETTING THERE tram 40 or 41 to Weinhauser Gasse
ACCESS by appointment

Hans Hollein 1990

Hans Hollein 1990

Management Book Service

When you enter you see only books – a good sign for a bookshop. Only tucked away right at the back you find some self-conscious pieces of 'design', a wall of thin curved concrete panels with impressions of leaves left in the concrete. In front of the leaves floats a book display, in front of the book display a long settee divided by small plywood tables, in front of the settee a bookshelf. A mirror extends this surprising little reading space back again into the shop. All is made of varnished furnitureboard, the floor covered with a grey standard needlefelt. The back office of the shop is open and you can see and hear book-business going on. Through the middle of the entire shop, right up the steps, run a long set of tables which hold books in different ways, under glass, in tall stacks, on shelves, on thin sheets of concrete. Only at the ends of the long table, where the cash tills are, does 'design' suddenly appear again under your elbow in the form of a small leather-upholstered shelf. Servus!

ADDRESS 9., Augasse 5–7 [20 L 11]
CLIENT Flicher, Scheidinger, Dagal, Strobi
GETTING THERE tram D to Augasse
ACCESS open

Eichinger oder Knechtl 1993

Eichinger oder Knechtl 1993

Fernwärme Wien

A painted shed.

ADDRESS 9., Spittelauer Lände 43 [20 L 11]
GETTING THERE tram D to Liechtenwerder Platz
ACCESS by guided tour in the Hundertwasser-style bus

Friedensreich Hundertwasser 1990

Alsergrund, Währing, Döbling

Friedensreich Hundertwasser 1990

Muthgasse

This small rental office building, next to Neumann's offices in a refurbished electricity works from 1897, was developed by the architect himself. It covers a narrow strip of the old site, stretching back from the road and forming a courtyard with the existing building. A solid blank wall faces the empty lot next door, and the offices look out on the lawn and the old building. The only thing breaking up the long stretch of windows is the glazed staircase and the orange cut in the facade which signals the entrance, one breaking out and the other breaking in, a single logical event in the long plain front.

It is too bad that more architects are not in a financial position to take this kind of risk, because the resulting quality of design and execution is way ahead of most other speculative office buildings. This is not because of expensive finishes or extravagant technology: the building is economically constructed on a simple plan. What impresses is the fine balance of the matter-of-factness of the materials – grey concrete block only embellished with five orange stripes of brick, galvanised steel and grey aluminium windows – and the attention given to their execution, coarse but considered.

ADDRESS 19., Muthgasse 107 [20 K 11]
REFURBISHMENT OF ELECTRICITY WORKS Neumann & Steiner
CLIENT Heinz Neumann
SIZE 4600 square metres
OTHER Adolf Loos Prize for Architecture 1993
GETTING THERE U4 or U6 to Heiligenstadt, then bus 38A to Mooslackengasse
ACCESS none

Heinz Neumann 1993

Gatterburggasse

There are relatively few architects who have been able to use the current housing boom to develop an expressed attitude to the organisation of modern life. Anton Schweighofer is one of the exceptions. He has defined an ideal plan-type, which is implemented with variations in many of his recent projects for inner city as well as in suburban housing. The plan uses the geometrical discipline of a square to provide an environment which can be inhabited in a variety of ways. This ideal square is organised into four equal undesignated rooms, one in each corner around a central space. Each of these four corner rooms could be a bedroom, a living room, a dining room, or any other kind of room to suit the needs of the occupant. Between these four large corner rooms are four smaller spaces containing the specialised serviced areas, the kitchen, the bathroom, the entrance hall with wc. All rooms are connected with the central space which can also be used in any number of ways – dining, working, open for circulation, receptions, playroom – depending on the life of the people living there. The plan is ingenious: practical, economical and open to interpretation. Rather than imposing restrictions, the strict geometry provides a framework for choice, while retaining a sense of privacy or a differentiation of areas of life which is often lost in a completely open plan.

In the project in Gatterburggasse this plan is implemented also on a larger scale; the internal courtyard between the two buildings repeats the interior central space. On both sides the courtyard is enclosed by glazed common staircases, a mature tree in the middle is the focus of both. In each corner of the overall plan are the individual flats, adapted to their different situations: orientated to the street or to the garden, incorporating terraces at the top or extended by loggias at the back. The geometry is a supporting structure, not an aim in itself. Between the flats the supporting spaces contain the street entrance, the staircases, and the

Anton Schweighofer 1989

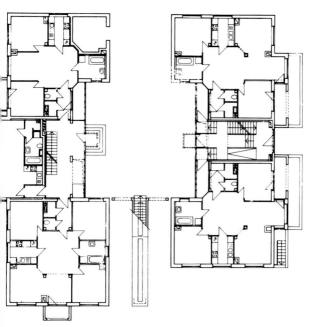

Anton Schweighofer 1989

entrance to the underground carpark and the garden. From the street the buildings appear as a white, solid box, unified by the simple shape of the curved roof, but then the internal courtyard, which is usually at the back of a city block, is pulled forward and presents something new to the street, a semi-private intermediate room for coming and going, repeating at an urban level the possibilities of the interior.

Alsergrund, Währing, Döbling

ADDRESS 19., Gatterburggasse 2C [20 K 11]
CLIENT Gemeinde Wien
SIZE 19 units
GETTING THERE tram 37 or 38 to Gatterburggasse
ACCESS to court

Anton Schweighofer 1989

Anton Schweighofer 1989

Grinzinger Allee 18

According to the long-term area plan for Vienna, Grinzinger Allee starts just where the dense city core comes to an end, and continues in a broad line through green gardens and villas to the historic village of Grinzing, to vineyards and the Wienerwald. The two new office buildings at the city end of Grinzinger Allee, one by Ulrike Janowetz and one by Heinz Neumann, have both made interesting use of their transitory position on the intersection between city and suburb.

Janowetz's modest three-storey building shields the garden behind with a formal white screen wall to the street. At the back the offices open to the neighbouring houses and gardens. Two glazed prows break through the back wall, one housing the staircase, the other with meeting rooms and canteen: the social part of office life is open to trees and sun, exposed within the protection of the domestic surroundings in a way which would not have been possible in a denser city situation. The glass also wraps around the side of the building and pokes through at the front, the corner detail clearly defining the front wall as a barrier device against the wide busy road.

ADDRESS 19., Grinzinger Allee 18
[19 J 10]
GETTING THERE tram 38 to
Sieveringer Strasse
ACCESS to entrance hall

Ulrike Janowetz 1991

Ulrike Janowetz 1991

Grinzinger Allee

This little mixed-use development of shops, offices and flats at the cross-over between dense urban and green suburban surroundings, reacts to its location in a similar way to the building by Ulrike Janowetz across the street. The flats and offices are shielded from the road by a clearly defined screen of glass and aluminium. The agent's site board in front declared it 'a milestone for Grinzinger Allee', reminding potential customers of 'the value of beauty' as a selling point for this uncompromisingly modern-looking development.

The façade materials are a refreshing sight, despite the fact that the general contractor has changed a lot of the final details, replacing what should have been clear edges and thin profiles with heavier, more standard solutions. The staircase for example, set on the front of the building like a major showpiece, is now a crude square protrusion with heavy standard profiles and thick concrete landings.

The building is divided into shops on the ground floor, offices on first and flats above, screened by the front wall and opening onto the footways and hedged lawns of other housing schemes to the back. The shops and offices prevent the flats from having direct access to the garden, but this is made up for by large balconies to all flats, glass and galvanised steel giving it a standard kind of elegance. All nicely dimensioned, clean and simple.

ADDRESS 19., Grinzinger Allee 3 [19 J 10]
CLIENT Ritter Vermögensverwaltung
SIZE 1500 square metres
GETTING THERE tram 38 to Sieveringer Strasse
ACCESS none

Heinz Neumann 1994

Gräf und Stift

With the rapid development of the building industry in Vienna, it is increasingly rare for site supervision to be the task of the architect. Although the situation is improving, site control is more often than not in the hands of technicans for whom the architect's drawings are little more than recommendations, resulting in discrepancies between intention and execution which makes any consistency very difficult. To overcome the problems of compromise, architects opt for the lowest common denominator right from the start, using only the limited range of details which the contractors are already used to.

Twenty-five architects contributed to the development of the former Gräf und Stift site, named after its former occupant, a vehicle manufacturer. In the end they did not have the site supervision and the execution of the building varies significantly from the design, particularly in the case of Helmut Richter and Heidulf Gerngross's project which was originally designed using another method of construction. However, the result in their case is still miles ahead of most mid-1980s' housing schemes, built at a time when the Viennese were still largely suffering under the yoke of mediocre post-modernism put together by large commercial practices of architects with political connections.

Richter and Gerngross's long terrace makes use of the natural drop in the site to give privacy to the ground-floor flats. On the street side an artificial plateau is made by communal facilities like bin- and bicycle stores. Balconies of painted steelwork and wired glass hang on the walls above, steering well clear of the empty decoration of many of the other schemes.

Anton Schweighofer's two blocks on either side of the little wedge-shaped piazza look more conventional, but the steelwork balconies, half coming out of the façade and half pulled in to the flats, are another of Schweighofer's inventions for modern housing. Inside, the balconies are

Various architects 1987–88

Various architects 1987–88

pulled into the plan like wintergardens, connected to the living spaces by interior glazed walls. Outside, the steel constructions stretch up the full height of the front of the building, giving a formal first impression which protects the space behind, where the half-withdrawn structures covered in plants are filled with the paraphernalia of domestic life.

Alsergrund, Währing, Döbling

ADDRESS 19., Weinberggasse 70–74 [19 J 9/10]
CLIENT Gemeinde Wien
GETTING THERE tram 38 to Oberdöbling, then bus 39A to Daringergasse
ACCESS to grounds

Various architects 1987–88

Hackenberggasse

Many of Vienna's new housing areas, particularly those designed by several architects, suffer from lack of attention to the landscaping, to the connecting areas between the individual building objects. Günther Oberhofer's four housing blocks at the edge between the city and the vineyards of Sievering are a successful exception. This is partly forced by the site, which slopes in both directions and demands active decisions about the relationship of the building to the ground: the steps between the four blocks are negotiated by a sequence of little round courtyards. Private gardens are set behind loggias of tall columns which give an effective intermediate scale and add to the impression of a unified whole taking account of its surroundings. The proximity of the private gardens and the semi-private circular courts, open to the public street, also brings the in-between areas into play on a social level. The tall columns are repeated on the corners of the street front, outlining a geometry which diverts the attention away from the large areas of glazing in the rooms behind. At first glance these concrete structures and the repeated chunky geometry of the street façades protect the privacy of the flats and the gardens, but behind them everything is open to view, giving the whole scheme a strange coyness, which rather than protect itself invites you to sneak a look.

ADDRESS 19., Hackenberggasse 17–19/Raimund-Zoder-Gasse
10–16 [19 J 9]
CLIENT SEG
SIZE 3400 square metres; 29 units
COST gross öS 56.6 million
GETTING THERE U6 to Nußdorfer Strasse, then bus 35A to Gustav-Pick-Gasse
ACCESS none

Alsergrund, Währing, Döbling

Günther Oberhofer 1990

Günther Oberhofer 1990

Basler Versicherungen office centre

The Donaukanal, the smaller side-channel to the new Donau, is a strangely underemphasised element in the architecture of Vienna. It is mostly edged by grey areas of undistinguished 19th-century housing, the monotony broken here and there by exceptions like Otto Wagner's weir-house and train station, a 1988 school by Carl Pruscha, the turn-of-the-century Urania by Max Fabiani. However, the banks of the Donaukanal have been occupying the planners since the 1970s, and now finally in the 1990s investors are starting to move in, and contemporary architects with them. It remains to be seen whether the will exists to realise Zaha Hadid's plans for the site below Hundertwasser's heating plant, but the new office building by Boris Podrecca is undeniably there, a shiny pearl in the grey riverfront of the 20th district.

The building is considerate in its connection to and extension of the urban structure of the area. It consists of a U-shaped building with an inner courtyard, completing a city block. The façade on Treugasse, away from the river, is a rendered wall of regular windows facing the existing buildings, open at ground level allowing people through to the riverbank on the other side. The internal courtyard is the end of the Othmargasse axis, which finally connects the river to the Brigitta Church, a welcome urban gesture in the even texture of housing blocks. The ground floor also has spaces for future shops and cafés.

But as much as it makes concessions to its modest surroundings, there is no mistaking the building's more glamorous intentions. The river frontage is a gleaming stretch of glass, clad in a pattern of green and a pale purple, colours extracted from the muddy run of the Donaukanal. The corner is a sheet of black polished granite, a flying shield lifted carefully just off the ground. The courtyard is crossed by bright red stripes taken up the wall by the columns and window mullions. The building is

Boris Podrecca 1993

Boris Podrecca 1993

a controlled bringing together of different parts, in a strongly graphic way particular to Podrecca. This graphic way of making architecture, with strong colours and geometrical cut-and-paste façades can very easily fall into simple decoration, but the river front and courtyard of this building is an impressive *tour-de-force* where a constant displacement and repetition from surface to surface of colour, of texture, of shape succeeds in making resonance, making space.

Alsergrund, Währing, Döbling

ADDRESS 20., Brigittenauer Lände 50–54 [20 K 11]
CLIENT Basler Immobilien
SIZE 22,000 square metres, 446 parking spaces
GETTING THERE tram 5 to Wallensteinstrasse
ACCESS to court and restaurant

Boris Podrecca 1993

Alsergrund, Währing, Döbling

Boris Podrecca 1993

Floridsdorf

Brünner Strasse

Look out for the stretch along Brünner Strasse. This area is designated for city expansion, and schemes to house 15,000 people are going up along the planned extension of the U6 between Floridsdorf and the new centre in Stammersdorf. Most of the area is under construction and difficult to evaluate, but one thing is certain: it will be big. The large expanses of housing blocks may have fewer storeys and brighter colours than was usual in the 1960s and '70s, but there is little to indicate that they embody any significant changes in social attitude. We shall see.

The project of Wimmer *et al*, however, falls outside this category. Firstly the site is situated much further in, towards the centre of Floridsdorf in a denser urban situation, and it deals with its site in a more determined way than the green-field developments further out. A full-length, full-height stretch of glazed balconies faces a park to the southwest, across from an old municipal swimming baths. The building meets the ground with a bright red rendered base, housing a supermarket on Brünner Strasse and sloped inwards to give half a storey's protection to the lower floor balconies. The entrance solution is lovely, a wide flight of stairs narrowing up to an entrance hall open to the garden behind. At the top of the block wide louvres on steel fins shade the top-floor terraces. The corner to Brünner Strasse is prised open and comes to an acute point, dividing the façade into a closed part towards the heavily trafficked Brünner Strasse and the glazed wall facing the park.

ADDRESS 21., Brünner Strasse 31/Gerichtsgasse 12 [9 G 14]
CLIENT GSG
SIZE 93 units, total 3500 square metres
GETTING THERE tram 31 from Schottenring to Schlingermarkt
ACCESS none

Helmut Wimmer, Eva Reich with P Zauchenberger and K Koller 1993

Floridsdorf

Helmut Wimmer, Eva Reich with P Zauchenberger and K Koller 1993

Die Ganze Woche

Unfortunately, industrial building has not benefited from the same informed commissioning as housing and other public buildings in recent years. One would hope that if and when investment in industry increases, city politicians will have set an example of the benefits of quality architecture. However, this printing works for *Täglich Alles* is one of the few recent examples of industrial buildings done by top-level architects.

The building is surprisingly modest in comparison with the tabloid paper it produces. The main spectacular part is the three floors of offices protruding above the entrance rotunda, shot out into the world balanced on tiny drums of solid metal atop four enormous concrete columns. The façade slopes out, thinly traced by the steel edge of the roof. There are some sharp things going on, but one is a little bit at a loss to see why; the huge effort of the elephantine columns does not seem quite justified simply by the decision to separate the offices from the rest of the complex. Behind the columns production goes on in a landscape of large sheds, undistinguished if nicely made. Inside, the exterior precision of the industrial materials (galvanised steel, corrugated sheet) is somewhat cheapened by the sudden luxury of beech and chrome handrails and the ubiquitous glass lift, which rises from the entrance to the office floors but from which, unfortunately, you can see nothing. Overall, the strategic decisions are very nicely detailed, but show no sign of the idea itself having been modified during the process of design.

ADDRESS 21., Ignaz-Köck-Strasse/Lundenburgergasse [9 F 14]
CLIENT Kurt Falk
SIZE 19,000 square metres
GETTING THERE tram 31 from Schottenring to Shuttleworthstrasse
ACCESS by appointment

Floridsdorf

Heinz Neumann 1991

Floridsdorf

Heinz Neumann 1991

Anton-Böck-Gasse

This intelligent housing project is located in Strebersdorf, on the very edge of the city, where the development from one- or two-storey rural buildings never quite happened. The site for the project is relatively large compared to many in the inner districts, but height restrictions and no doubt financial considerations have necessitated a higher site coverage than is traditional for the area. This has resulted in a compact sequence of differently identified spaces and elements which tie the different buildings together in a complex whole.

The façade to Anton-Böck-Gasse is simple and smooth, grey render and in-situ concrete balconies. The first layer in the sequence of entry is a slender galvanised steel structure on the façade which supports maturing climbing plants, connecting the new building to the well-groomed private houses in the surrounding area. The façade itself is carefully differentiated by the irregular distribution of flat surface, closed and open balconies, projecting and recessed windows. This full glazing of balconies is a trick to get around the regulations governing the small proportion of window to wall you are allowed in social house building: a balcony it is not counted as a habitable room, which it can nonetheless become, at least for a large proportion of the year. From the street the building looks deceptively small, only opening up once you pass the communal children's playroom above the double-height entrance to stand underneath the mature tree in the first courtyard. The generous site allows a progression of entry and gradual engagement which you don't often find in tighter situations: from street past façade through entrance hall to internal courtyard to gallery to garden beyond.

Inside, what holds the dense complex together are the differences between its various elements: here the concrete is painted red but not there, here there is glass, here a concrete pergola, here yellow wood

Eva Ceska and Friedrich Priesner 1993

Floridsdorf

Eva Ceska and Friedrich Priesner 1993

around an entrance door, here aluminium; here black and white terrazzo. The simple materials and coarse but elegant detailing, consistent with the given conditions of social housing, have not been allowed to limit the possibilities of spatial differentiation and refinement. The consistent and minimal detailing also prevents the various parts from pulling in opposite directions – there is none of the determined confusion of, for example, Hollein's school in Köhlergasse (see page 226). Rather, the identification of differences, in such close proximity to each other, gives a strong sense of localised identity: I live on a gallery, under the roof, in the garden; I enter through glass, along a red wall, up a stair; I live here and not anywhere else. The clients got a lot of good architecture for their money.

ADDRESS 21., Anton-Böck-Gasse 4 [1 D 13]
CLIENT 'Frieden'
STRUCTURAL ENGINEER Johann Sittner
SIZE 57 units, total 4440 square metres
GETTING THERE tram 32 to Edmund-Hawranek-Platz or s3 to Strebersdorf, then bus 32A to Anton-Böck-Gasse
ACCESS none

Floridsdorf

Eva Ceska and Friedrich Priesner 1993

Floridsdorf

Eva Ceska and Friedrich Priesner 1993

Praterstern to Essling, Donaustadt

IBM Office Centre

At first glance, Holzbauer's three buildings on Lasallestrasse are very similar in terms of materials, scale, and bulk, and are invariably judged as one. On closer inspection differences quickly become apparent and, more interestingly, reveal a lot about the organisations the buildings were made for.

IBM is a modern, self-conscious company with very clear business ideals. IBM only has a 15-year lease on the site, but the close fit of the building to the organisation ensures maximum efficiency and is very different from the much more conventional Bank Austria building opposite (see page 268). The first design priority was that each employee should have their own window. As a result the building has a zig-zag plan with large chunks gouged out of the main form, giving 500 metres of façade. The windows are shaped to give a darker background for computer screens. Meeting rooms are open to the corridor, some occupying the windowless areas in the middle to keep meetings shorter. There is always light at the end of a corridor so you can orientate yourself intuitively in the building, and in the larger circulation areas you can always see the Big Wheel in the Prater, giving you orientation within the city. Lifts are tucked away to the side on the ground floor to encourage employees to use the stairs.

From the outside the building looks larger than it is. The atriums are disguised by large beams which complete the theoretical form of the building, and the lack of external detailing belies the modest seven storeys.

IHA: How do you deal with, or do you mind, the image you have of being 'the architect who does the big things'?
Wilhelm Holzbauer: Look ... personally I find it so ridiculous. You prob-

Praterstern to Essling, Donaustadt

Wilhelm Holzbauer et al 1992

Praterstern to Essling, Donaustadt

Wilhelm Holzbauer et al 1992

ably know Liesebeth Waechter-Böhm …

IHA: Not personally but I read her critiques in *Die Presse* …

Holzbauer: Well, first in the Kärntnerringhof she counted how many tonnes of stone are in the building, and how many lamps, and she took it as being bad that so many tonnes of stone went into it. And for the Bank Austria she had the headline: 'Too big to be good'.

IHA: The only reason I can think for saying something like that is that your buildings are also big on a small scale. They are big, I don't mind that they're big, but when you do such big projects there's a certain level of detail, a certain quality which obviously is impossible to achieve.

Holzbauer: Well, have you been in the hall in the Bank Austria?

IHA: No, not yet.

ADDRESS 2., Lasallestrasse 1 [33 M 13]
CLIENT IBM
ASSOCIATED ARCHITECTS K Hlawenizcka, A Lintl, H Glück, G Lippert
GETTING THERE U1 to Praterstern
ACCESS by appointment

Wilhelm Holzbauer et al 1992

Praterstern to Essling, Donaustadt

Wilhelm Holzbauer et al 1992

Bank Austria I and II

Bank Austria was formed by the fusion of two major Austrian banks in 1991. Eager to establish its presence in the city, it has used architecture very consciously as a means to this end. However, in comparison to the IBM building, the Bank Austria office centres appear awkward and monolithic. The entrances signal the difference in approach: at IBM a long, light canopy protrudes into the world; Bank Austria is entered through a stone arch along a five-storey polished stone wall. The bank's brief specified 11 square metres per person, with no qualitative requirements. The employees are placed in large offices of three or four people, or in open-plan offices. The offices are placed along double internal corridors running the entire 130 metres of the block. Cabling to the desk positions comes up in the middle of the room, so it is impossible to place desks by the window. You orientate yourself by a system of numbers and colour coding, but because the staff are moving around, the colours keep changing, and are only indicated by little plaques next to the doors; the carpets, for example, are a uniform grey-purple throughout.

The bank has bought a standard shell, without making use of the services of the architect to define what the organisation itself is all about. This despite the fact that they have bought the ground and the house and presumably are there for life rather than a quick sting of 15 years.

Holzbauer: I think the level of detailing is quite good, the glass wall, the steelwork, I think the standard of detailing is quite high.

IHA: You included, I noticed, in the back of one of your books, a poem about you by Coop Himmelblau, 'Der Fürst' (The Prince).

Holzbauer: Yes, that's right. They wrote it for me, and we included it.

IHA: I thought that was very sweet. Is your role like that?

Holzbauer: Ja … in a way.

Wilhelm Holzbauer et al 1993 and 1994

Wilhelm Holzbauer et al 1993 and 1994

IHA: It is not a position that you particularly aspire to or actively build up?

Holzbauer: No. Certainly not. Frankly, I don't care what image I transport.

IHA: Also not through your buildings?

Holzbauer: Well. I would say it really doesn't affect me too much how it is received, because on the other hand I must say that the users of my buildings are almost always very happy. This is something which gives me a great deal of satisfaction. And the people from IBM, from what I hear, are all very satisfied.

Praterstern to Essling, Donaustadt

ADDRESS 2., Lasallestrasse 5 [33 M 13]
ASSOCIATED ARCHITECTS K Hlawenizcka, A Lintl, H Glück, G Lippert
STRUCTURAL ENGINEERS Fiolich, Körner & Werner
SIZE 54,000 square metres
GETTING THERE U1 to Praterstern
ACCESS by appointment

Wilhelm Holzbauer et al 1993 and 1994

Wilhelm Holzbauer et al 1993 and 1994

Donau-Zentrum extension

One of the problems of developing large areas of housing in a short time is that they lack habits. Planners usually deal with this by installing 'local centres' in the outer districts, a policy which inevitably centres around traffic roundabouts or shopping. These artificial town centres, pacemakers of urban life, are easy enough to build and to sell, but they cannot construct overnight in the public mind the patterns formed in an old city centre by years of urban habits. Copying old urban shapes does not help. Points of public attraction appear slowly; only with use do patterns emerge, and they are impossible to predict in a strategic area plan.

The centre at the end of the U1 is one of these artificial nodes. It is an important interchange for the whole of the 22nd district: the unearthly sleek shell of the U-bahn streaks in overhead, buses and trams circle incessantly. In the middle of this, Marschalek & Ladstätter's shopping and office complex has landed confidently between the bus stop and the old Donau-Zentrum. The architects have challenged the area's lack of scale with a horizontal division of the façade and careful detailing. The huge car park is beautifully shielded by two access ramps, wrapped in a precise spiralling layer of steel mesh, benign in spite of their impossible function. All this, and it is still a large, introverted solid-block shopping centre – caught between the preconceptions of planners and the predictable priorities of financial interests, the building fails to give the area a soul.

ADDRESS 22., Wagramer Strasse [21 L 14]
CLIENT Ekazent Realitätengesellschaft mbH
SIZE 14,200 square metres of shops, 850 parking spaces
COST ÖS 364 million
GETTING THERE U1 to Kagran
ACCESS open

Praterstern to Essling, Donaustadt

Heinz Marschalek and Georg Ladstätter with Alfred Beck 1986

Praterstern to Essling, Donaustadt

Heinz Marschalek and Georg Ladstätter with Alfred Beck 1986

Heinrich-Lefler-Gasse

Where the tram line passes to the north of this block, you look one way into brightly lit streets lined with shops, the other way out across small industrial sheds to the open fields of Aspern. On this edge, where the city changes and begins to grow dense, Michael Loudon has designed a very elegant apartment building. Loudon has a history of challenging the preconceptions of social housing with his participation projects in Bregenz and Sulz. He does it with a natural simplicity which goes beyond the aesthetics of minimalism and the patronising construction systems of self build; it is the through the spaces, the architecture, rather than through the icons of user participation, that Loudon's buildings achieve their inhabitability. In Heinrich-Lefler-Gasse you can sense such architecture at a hundred paces. The simple rendered façade is opened by rows of wide, strangely proportioned windows. These large windows are hinged on a centre pivot, and as they are opened the whole façade changes according to the use of the rooms behind. The windows and balconies were originally intended to be covered by sliding glass screens, which would have made what Loudon calls this 'architecture indicative of collective use' more expressive, but no Viennese architect seems to escape that final round of value engineering.

The plan is a formidable achievement. Similar to Schweighofer's ideal geometry, Loudon has managed to get the client to pay for nothing, to pay for undefined areas open to the interpretation of use. The services are arranged in a strip through the centre of the long block, and each flat is entered through an ambivalent zone which can be 'a corridor, a winter garden, a loggia or an extension of the living space' (Michael Loudon, *Fenster und Korridore/Windows and Corridors*, Wien 1992), separated only by sliding glazed screens. The flats to the back of the block incorporate a similar zone in the middle of the plan between bedroom and

Michael Loudon 1994

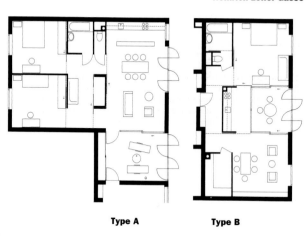

Type A   **Type B**

Michael Loudon 1994

living room. The interior is divided by sliding doors, giving the option of a very open plan connecting all the spaces along the front façade, kitchen into dining into living, or the conventional arrangement of divided rooms. This degree of flexibility within the framework of subsidised housing is a formidable achievement.

In my quest for generalities within the wide range of current housing construction, I would propose that this is an area where a common attitude is traceable in the best of what is being built: a social attitude to architecture which goes beyond the ideological wishful thinking of sadly disused communal rooms, an attitude which accepts and gives dignity and expression to individual choice within a social structure.

ADDRESS 22., Heinrich-Lefler-Gasse 24 [35 M 17]
CLIENT 'Neues Leben'
SIZE 28 units
GETTING THERE U1 to Kagran, then tram 25 to Hardeggasse
ACCESS none

Michael Loudon 1994

Michael Loudon 1994

Zschokkegasse

Next to Rainer's dense low courtyard (see page 280) lies this huge four-storey fortress with green steel windows, green painted details and external timberwork. The building is a contained complex of internal covered courtyards with balconies and terraces for the flats, alternating with open passages through internal gardens. It is symmetrical and ordered, and the open private balconies overhead, covered with flowering plants, give the inner courts a dense social atmosphere.

The problem of city expansion in areas like this is that there is nothing there but green fields, and architect after architect can freely put their objects down – very few areas have been given a larger structure which can be extended or developed. A loose agglomeration of single projects spreads rapidly across the available land. The environment is largely man-made, but there seems to be no decision as to whether it should be really dense, like the city proper, or connected to the land, making use of the opportunities which that gives. It is too early to judge social success, it is all developing so fast – but, for example, is it a conscious city-planning decision to have a Hufnagl project next to one by Rainer?

ADDRESS 22., Zschokkegasse 91 [35 M 17]
CLIENT EBG
SIZE 55 + 59 + 59 units
GETTING THERE U1 to Kagran, tram 25 to Sozialmedizinisches Zentrum Ost
ACCESS none

Viktor Hufnagl 1992

Viktor Hufnagl 1992

Siedlung Tamariskengasse

In contrast to the surrounding 1970s' four- to five-storey blocks, Roland Rainer has implemented his philosophy of suburban building: dense and low. His project is a field of one- and two-storey single-family houses, each with its own walled courtyard, shielded from the prevailing winds by long three-storey blocks to the north and west. The field is organised around two long pedestrian squares connected by a long wedge-shaped lawn. All cars are relegated to the double underground garage, leaving the stark tiled areas between the buildings for pedestrians only, another of Rainer's strong convictions. The buildings are white and simple, a sharp accusation against the vaguely mediocre post-modern façades of the surrounding blocks.

ADDRESS 22., Tamariskengasse 102 [35 M 18]
CLIENT GESIBA
SIZE 96 flats, 77 two-storey terraced houses, 59 atrium houses
GETTING THERE U1 to Kagran, tram 25 to Sozialmedizinisches Zentrum Ost
ACCESS to grounds

Praterstern to Essling, Donaustadt

Roland Rainer 1993

Roland Rainer 1993

Kapellenweg

This building on bland, suburban Kapellenweg is waiting for the city to arrive. Five storeys of terracotta and lavender grey, 200 metres long, with a lookout at either end searching the horizons of the 22nd district for signs of approaching urbanity. There is something strange about developments of this scale and density appearing round the perimeter of the city; they appear unattached, their form and colour taken from somewhere outside the immediate surroundings. Irreproachably symmetrical, precisely proportioned, Podrecca's block is one of these outposts. The flats are an imaginative mixture of single level, triple level with a gallery, and maisonettes at the top, with balconies and terraces as the block steps back from the façade, from white to red to grey.

Very soon these slender 200 metres will be dwarfed by the enormous development being constructed next door; 37 cranes tower over the field at Langobardenstrasse at the time of writing. Has the city finally arrived? Or is the 22nd district becoming the storeroom of Vienna, for people, for architectural styles, a scoreboard for political points? All the new buildings, including that by Podrecca, are so self-contained, so self-sufficient in their function and their architecture, as if no future changes, additions or subtractions, would be possible, as if no context ever existed. It is hard to imagine that all these singularities will ever come together in something that can be identified as a city.

ADDRESS 22., Kapellenweg 36–38 [35 M 18]
CLIENT ÖS
SIZE 80 units, total 15,300 square metres
COST total ÖS 200 million
GETTING THERE U3 to Schlachthausgasse, then bus 84A to Kapellenweg
ACCESS to grounds

Boris Podrecca/Gotthard Eiböck 1992

Boris Podrecca/Gotthard Eiböck 1992

Siedlung Pilotengasse

The long rows of Siedlung Pilotengasse stretch out across a flat field, no trees, no undulations, no shade and no landscape other than the houses themselves. The subtly curved terraces concentrate around an invisible centre, clearly distinguished from their surroundings – the most important context appears to be the horizon and the sky above. The grey rows to the west are by Herzog & De Meuron, the ones at the centre by Steidle, and the most brightly coloured ones to the east by Krischanitz.

By now the unfamiliar forms and impossibly bright colours of the buildings have grown into a dense even field of domestic life, all blow-up paddling pools and garden furniture. Because the rows of repeated units are so close, they are mercilessly exposed to each other, willed together in an unnatural proximity which the bright colours can only partly detract from. The long even stretches of wall have no intermediate spaces, only tiny wire fences divide the individual gardens. As housing this scheme poses a social as well as an architectural challenge, which becomes very visible as people fill it.

IHA: Did the social program of Pilotengasse change the way you …

Adolf Krischanitz: Yes. It wasn't possible to do all the things we wanted to do, but it was important in that it's a normally financed settlement with subsidies and a very low budget. Our credo was to avoid the post-modern small city-image; a Siedlung is a Siedlung is a Siedlung, *not* a small village. At the time most people had some romantic influence in their work, they were trying to construct this lie of a happy world. I think our programme at the time was to do a normal settlement, and our work since has been influenced by this experience.

IHA: You like it hard, you like it controversial, clearly cut – is there a reaction in that to this city and its traditions?

Adolf Krischanitz, Herzog & De Meuron, Otto Steidle & Partner 1992

Pratenstern to Essling, Donaustadt

Adolf Krischanitz, Herzog & De Meuron, Otto Steidle & Partner 1992

Krischanitz: Yes. But it's also not possible to have such a clear picture of what is done and what is to do. It is only possible to have a commission and to work, and to react in this work. And in the next work you have to react in a different way. It's like a game which can be played more-or-less intelligently. Sometimes architecture is important for other people, sometimes not.

IHA: Is architecture a marginal occupation?

Krischanitz: We can work a very long time on a problem and it looks normal, and we can work a very short time on a problem and it looks abnormal, but sometimes it can look so normal that it becomes a scandal, and maybe I quite like that. Not the scandal in itself, but I like to work towards finding a solution which is direct, to spring it on the point. On the other hand I see that this finest point is very dangerous to some people.

IHA: Do you think you need a particular education to understand contemporary architecture?

Krischanitz: Not so much. I see that people react very strongly to my architecture. It's not important that they say it's wonderful. It's important that they say 'what is it?'

ADDRESS 22, Pilotengasse [35/36 M 18/19]
CLIENT ÖS
ENGINEER Dworak Röder
SIZE 201 units, 21 types
COST ÖS 327 million
GETTING THERE U1 to Kagran, then bus 26A to Obersdorfstrasse
ACCESS general

Adolf Krischanitz, Herzog & De Meuron, Otto Steidle & Partner 1992

Adolf Krischanitz, Herzog & De Meuron, Otto Steidle & Partner 1992

Siedlung Siegesplatz/Benjowskigasse

Three different building types make the transition from single-storey rural building on Siegesplatz to the larger villas on Benjowskigasse, through an internal street of terraced houses. Passing under the tiled roof to Siegesplatz you go through two red internal courtyards, along vibrant blue curved timber fencing in front of the terrace to the fragmented deep pink blocks at the back. There are galvanised steel mailboxes, lamp posts, etc, carefully detailed, there are fibreboard-clad porches with plastic screwcaps, poured asphalt on the internal street, pebbled ditches along the housewalls – familiar materials used in reassuringly unfamiliar ways.

Rüdiger Lainer: For us it was a kind of experiment, trying to cross the boundary of how narrative you can be, to see how far you can go behind the project with all these narrative processes.

IHA: What do you mean, 'narrative'?

Lainer: There are a lot of stories behind the Siegesplatz project, about topography, geology, boundary, many non-visible stories determining how the buildings were orientated and how the house-forms came about. For the work we do now, it is not so interesting to repeat that process. I think it was stimulating and important, as I always thought that you can transfer this process into building, but what came out in the end is very much a form, which cannot be related to the stories or ideas behind it.

IHA: But the Aspern project sits very beautifully in the context of where it is?

Lainer: Part of the project was also to see how you could develop these old villages, to say OK, you make a boundary with the building at the end, and then extend the existing morphology – but there are a lot of other elements informing this project. I think it is very integrated, and

Rüdiger Lainer and Gertraud Auer 1991

Praterstern to Essling, Donaustadt

Rüdiger Lainer and Gertraud Auer 1991

in many ways I like it, but I think now I'm much more interested in, for example, the flexibility of floorplan and how the construction follows. What's interesting is not what's actual, but where you think you can learn: where you can make verification and falsification. Sometimes you're wrong, but you can learn a lot from the falsification too.

IHA: Is building necessary for architecture?

Lainer: Yes, I think so now. I did a lot of theoretical work before I started to build, and I realised there was a big gap between the theoretical thesis and the building process, which became an antithesis. This is an immanent problem in both politics and arcitecture. Peter Eisenman's building in Berlin, and that of Raimund Abraham, represent for me this gap that exists between theory and practice. Abraham produces beautiful drawings, but then in the transfer to building, all sensitivity is lost. It is not so much a gap between thinking and construction but more the idea of the two things forming part of a net where things are related, and you have to try to find the lines of the net through this constant process of verification and falsification. In that way the complexity of the thinking process can be transferred to architecture, into architectonics. As I said, in Aspern I consider that a lot of the narrative processes which went before are no longer legible, which was one of these falsifications for me.

ADDRESS 22, Siegesplatz 21/Benjowskigasse 11 [36 M 19]
CLIENT SEG
SIZE 21 units
COST ÖS 24 million
GETTING THERE U1 to Kagran, then bus 26A to Aspern Siegesplatz
ACCESS none

Rüdiger Lainer and Gertraud Auer 1991

Rüdiger Lainer and Gertraud Auer 1991

Siedlung Biberhaufenweg

The 22nd district is a major area for city expansion. The connections to the city centre through the U1 and the s-bahn are improving, there is plenty of open space – large areas of housing are being constructed on the greenfield sites in Süssenbrunn, Aspern and Essling, accompanied by schools and shopping centres, and there are more to come. The landscape is wide, flat – long roads, one-family houses, trees and open fields – a rural landscape where you can still see the horizon which is slowly being covered by the spreading city.

This undetermined city edge offers no models of its own for high-density building, and is rapidly developing a varied inventory of responses to the challenge of modern housing. There are mega-blocks going up on the Langobardenstrasse, there are Rainer's low and dense terraces, Hufnagl's courtyards, the much-publicised Pilotengasse by Krischanitz, Steidle and Herzog & De Meuron, and complex morphological experiments by Lainer/Auer. Each area is developed separately, by different architects and different clients, with only minimal detailed direction from the planning authorities. It is hard to tell what potential the area will have once it all starts to grow together; at the moment there is enough room for everyone to play their own game.

Siedlung Biberhaufenweg was one of the early architectural experiments in the area. The site is divided between three architects, each exploring a separate theme. Entrance to the site is through a narrow opening in one of the blocks enclosing Heinz Tesar's little Square. The scale is a modest two to three storeys, but the formality of the layout and the combination of fairfaced concrete elements and coarse white render shaped into little pitched porches and curved gables makes it clear that here is something which takes its architectural task seriously.

Off to the side is Otto Häuselmayer's short Street, a long block of flats

Heinz Tesar, Otto Häuselmayer, Carl Pruscha 1985

Heinz Tesar, Otto Häuselmayer, Carl Pruscha 1985

on one side and a terrace of houses on the other. It has the same self-conscious formality, symmetrical organisation and ceremonial little entrances, by now pleasantly contrasted by the mild disorder of Austrian domestic life – trees, toys, bins and bicycles.

Through the square lie the two rows of Carl Pruscha's Green, a sharply angled terrace shooting out towards the hazy fields beyond, the curves of the roofs drawn in sharp steel sheet against the sky, as if by the sea. All the houses are built in the same materials, concrete, render, timber window frames and sheet steel roofs, so the different themes of the three parts are set against each other in a polite, hushed conversation.

ADDRESS 22., Biberhaufenweg 15 [35 N 18]
GETTING THERE U1 to Kagran, then bus 26A to Aspern Siegesplatz or 93A to Asperner Heldenplatz
ACCESS to square

Heinz Tesar, Otto Häuselmayer, Carl Pruscha 1985

Heinz Tesar, Otto Häuselmayer, Carl Pruscha 1985

Wiethestrasse

The new housing area in Wiethestrasse, Essling, is a confident contribution to the growing catalogue of possibilities in contemporary subsidised housing.

The part by Fonatti & Hempel (A and D) is the most complex, a solid block to the front, opening a double-height glazed corner to the garden. The architects have stretched the finances of social housing to their limits to provide as much spatial and material variation as possible. Each unit has a private garage and guest parking at the front. There is no strict separation between cars and people, allowing the culture of the family car to come right up to the front door and be a part of the rituals of social life.

Gerngross (C) has taken the restrictions of normal social-housing construction as a starting point, and instead of pushing for expensive finishes he has tried to optimise the possibilities of making a generous internal space. The serviced parts are tightly organised in a central area, leaving a huge double-height living space to the front, which can be filled in with floors should the inhabitants' requirements change. The exteriors are rendered grey, with dark grey detailing. It seems stark in comparison to Fonatti & Hempel's scheme – is it enough to provide a neutral background for a life to come, or could the architect suggest possible associations?

The part by Weiser & Baldass (B) is the most conventional of the three: painting the entrance porches a strong colour is not really enough to make you ignore the small windows and deep-set balconies.

The external areas are divided by precise concrete walls. The part by Fonatti & Hempel has the advantage of a clear division between front and back which gives privacy to the gardens, Weiser & Baldass and particularly Gerngross have to contend with very exposed building positions allowing little privacy in the connection of inside to outside. This is a

Helmut Hempel (area plan) 1994

Praterstern to Essling, Donaustadt

Helmut Hempel (area plan) 1994

problem in most recent housing projects: even if the overall planning is done by one of the architects, the concern is inevitably for the building object. For whatever reason, the spaces inbetween are not really negotiated, they are accidental leftovers sown with grass, the main function of which appears to be keeping the various architects' solutions at a safe distance from each other. One of the results of this non-strategy is a strange sense of exposure around the houses: as soon as you step outside the walls you are in public view, there are no intermediate zones between inside and outside. Perhaps it is simply a question of time: the inhabitants will grow hedges, put up fences, playhouses and barbecues, but the architects usually provide little structure for the use of external space.

ADDRESS 22., Wiethestrasse 84 [37 N 21]
ARCHITECTS Franco Fonatti & Helmut Hempel (parts A and D), Heinz H Weiser & Georg Baldass (part B), and Heidulf Gerngross (part C)
CLIENT GSG
STRUCTURAL ENGINEER Albert Röder
PROJECT MANAGEMENT Werkstatt Wien
SIZE A 19 units, each 129 square metres; B 33, C 26 and D 12 units
GETTING THERE U1 to Kagran, then bus 26A to Eßling Schule
ACCESS to grounds

Helmut Hempel (area plan) 1994

Pappelweg

A simple long terrace of uniform grey rendered houses with façade panels of white timber boarding. Each unit is symmetrical around its own axis, refreshingly unspectacular and well-organised. From the road you can see through the open living space on the ground floor to the path at the back. The plans, despite the narrow frontage, are open and generous.

A tight path runs along the back where the entrances are, the gardens face west, on to the street, divided only by thin stretches of galvanised steel mesh. A clear structure limited to its plot, with no pretenses, hugely popular with its inhabitants.

ADDRESS 22., Pappelweg 1–34 [35 N 17]
SIZE ten flats, 27 terraced houses
GETTING THERE U1 to Kagran, then tram 25 to Erzherzog-Karl-Strasse and bus 96B to Kanalstrasse
ACCESS none

Roland Hagmüller 1992

Roland Hagmüller 1992

Kamillenweg

An experiment in ecological building visible in the construction of the houses, timber cladding with large south-facing atria, and in the layout of the whole. The part by Reinberg-Treberspurg-Raith (A) organises two blue timber terraces around a central sheltered area with a large fertile pond and a communal house with a large glass front, all connected by paved pedestrian paths. The north-facing slope of the roofs is covered with grass. The south-facing private gardens and the adjoining conservatories are filled with mature and flowering plants of all kinds, making it look like the whole scheme is inhabited by a society of horticulturalists – everywhere something is growing and it is very beautiful. Keith Collie was asked in by one man to look at his banana tree, which had really big clusters of bananas.

The parts by Kislinger & Trudak (B) are less straightforward, two-storey barracks glazed on one side with timber used more as a decorative element on the façade. The sense of a consistent sequence of decisions is lost behind the graphics of the façade.

ADDRESS 22., Kamillenweg/Pappelweg/Haßelnussweg [35 N 17]
CLIENT 'Neues Leben'
SITE SUPERVISION Werkstatt Wien
SIZE A 19 and B nine units plus communal house
GETTING THERE U1 to Kagran, then tram 25 to Erzherzog-Karl-Strasse, then bus 96B to Kanalstrasse
ACCESS to grounds

G Reinberg, M Treberspurg & E Raith, and Kislinger & Trudak 1992

Praterstern to Essling, Donaustadt

G Reinberg, M Treberspurg & E Raith, and Kislinger & Trudak 1992

Index

Vienna: a guide to recent architecture

Vienna: a guide to recent architecture

Vienna: a guide to recent architecture

Vienna: a guide to recent architecture

Vienna: a guide to recent architecture

Picture credits

Photographs by Keith Collie,
  except:
page 29 courtesy Helmut Richter
pages 39, 87, 89 courtesy Coop
  Himmelblau, photo Gerald
  Zugmann
page 41 courtesy Wolfgang
  Tschapeller
page 45 courtesy Eichinger oder
  Knechtl
page 75 courtesy Franziska
  Ullman, photo Margherita
  Spiluttini
page 118 courtesy Boris
  Podrecca, photo Gerald
  Zugmann
page 193 courtesy Elsa
  Prochazka, photo Margherita
  Spiluttini
page 203 courtesy Helmut
  Richter
page 247 courtesy Günther
  Oberhofer
page 281 courtesy Roland Rainer